MW01531188

My C.,
From
Carol

In Due Season
Destiny Is Calling Your Soul
By Carol S. Batey

ISBN: 9781461045298

In Due Season:
Destiny Is Calling Your Soul
A guide to discovering your soul's
purpose and
facilitating your personal
transformation.
One woman's insightful spiritual
journey of
reinventing herself and remembering
her destiny.

Carol Batey
Lifestyle Coach

Carol Batey's motivation to reach her fitness
goals is an inspiration that could definitely
motivate others. Readers will get ideas from
her exercise regimen that they could
incorporate into their own programs.
—Glenn Jamison, Physical Education Teacher and
Personal Trainer

Carol Batey,
author of Parents Are Lifesavers
Let's awaken your soul's purpose for your
ultimate potential on your life's journey.
It's now your season.

Table of Contents

I Give Thanks

With a warm thankful heart I acknowledge special friends who encouraged me to put my hand to a pencil and thoughts on paper for you the reader. Those special friends are Dr. Alciea Fair, Carolyn Parker, Gloria Sawyers, and Carol Clark. They all pushed the insightful development of In Due Season: Destiny is Calling Your Soul. They would not let me stop until I was finished! Blessings and love to them. A special kindness to Gina Griffins for her undivided attention and listening ear when I need to vent my ideas to her no matter what time of the day. There are many earthly angels that assist those on their spiritual paths. My editorial angels are knowledgeable; they are Laura Pugh, Cheri Wells, Dominique Allen, and Jeanmarie Martin, who put the finishing polish on this manuscript. All of them made this project copy-ready and user-friendly.

I give thanks to my integrated heritage and to the ancestors who left an imprint on the DNA of my soul. Many thanks for the real-life lessons taught to me by my six children and my grandbaby, Jaila. I want to thank my Sacred Source for guiding and directing me on my journey.

The Spirit allowed me to create my days!

Special affirming thanks for the support of the unique diverse spiritual community at Unity in Old Hickory, Tennessee. No spiritual community is strong without a spiritual leader. Reverend Denise Yeargin's Sunday nourishment for the soul blessed and uplifted me each week. Her inspiring messages confirmed to me what I knew in my heart to be true about the lessons of life while using Unity's teachings along with the inspiration of good books; all the while, Rev. Yeargin inspired and influenced my heart and mind to further understanding and knowledge while on my spiritual journey. She pushed me and fed me while teaching her message to live a fuller life in love for all humankind.

Finally, I thank Dr. Louise Mallory-Elliot for her insightful Christ-Conscious workshops I attended, in addition to the Law of Attraction with meditation. The workshops poured pure energy from Spirit into my body and gave me the fortitude to bring this book to fruition.

Introduction

Dearest Reader,

While meditating, creating, and writing this book for you, I held you in my heart and mind. *In Due Season: Destiny is Calling Your Soul* is an account of my personal transformation and purpose on this earth. The title *In Due Season* comes from the Bible, Galatians 6:9, *"And let not us grow weary (give up) while doing good, for in (the right) time we shall reap (yield what we have planted), if we do not lose heart (lose faith)."*

I put myself in your traveling shoes, covering the miles upon miles you will need to reach your ultimate inner goal or transformation. Many have asked how to identify the purpose of their journey. They have also asked how to make time to accomplish their purpose and where the money will come from. To uncover your personal transformation, you first start with a desire to create. Next, a spiritual practice of meditating, fasting and prayer, journaling, being still and listening, and physical exercising and proper nutrients will help you start your transformation.

As I examined my ego, my true desires for the reasons for wanting change came out, and I made a resolution to do the hard work necessary to get physically, spiritually, emotionally, and mentally fit. My goal was to become a new Carol. The labor and the miles traveled weren't as hard once I surrendered and gave into the Universal Spirit's laws. The principles and applications in this book are tried, tested, and proven true if your heart and soul are open and your spirit and mind are willing. I used them daily to achieve my desired outcomes for my soul's purpose and personal transformation. Every application may not be for your soul's change; think of whatever is needed for you.

With the Master Creator's divine help we can awaken our minds, bodies, and souls to remember our purpose. Seeking the Divine's help by asking for assistance from Spirit is where we start first, since we are co-creators in our destiny. Knocking down the walls of false ego and the barriers of protection we have built up over the years is second. Through a daily spiritual practice you can gain courage, faith, inner well-being, insights, humility, and directions and answers for your daily walk or journey.

Surrendering helps one to lose the false ego that doesn't serve anyone but the ego. Humility is developed and welcomed, and then Spirit's help is there to guide you on your course. You and I become co-creators with the Divine, God, our sacred source. God is a name that may be different for others. A few of the names for God include: The Deity, Krishna, Buddha, Mohammed, Jesus Christ, or others. There is an old wise saying that tells us there are many paths that lead to God. It's important that you learn to develop a trust and wisdom in a Higher Power greater than yourself.

As spirit beings on this earth you will face adverse conditions on your path, but don't look at a situation as right or wrong. Look past the objection and see the outcome you want to achieve. It is our earthly task to use our free will and discernment powers to move forward and not against the grain. Most problems aren't as they appear.

This book will begin your awakening. If you allow it, you will find buried treasure within your soul, spirit, and mind. Principles mentioned will nourish and direct your soul. Th en the power of God will start to transform your life. Spirit's guidance will be felt within your soul and around it, directing your path daily. Learn to let go, surrender to the Universal God and the Laws of the earth, "The Law of Attraction and Allowing." You will inherit joy, peace, wisdom, abundant living, and a new purpose in life. You will create unity with your God.

Love and peace,
Carol Batey

Chapter 1
My Soul's Transformation
"Thoughts held in mind, reproduce after their kind"
3rd Principle of the Unity Teachings

It's been said that health is not a commodity to be bargained for; it has to be earned. Recently I saw a book titled, *Health is by Choice, Not by Chance*. This book is not just about health concerns, but also about how to use your mind and your body to achieve your dreams. Are you now ready to unfold your soul's healthy lifestyle journey and uncover your life mission or purpose by reading about mine? It's all your choice, for you are a free agent who can make your own choices. When I approached my 50th birthday, I had a sound determination, real purpose, and
a creative personal plan to reach my healthy lifestyle goals and transform myself. According to the dictionary, the word *transform* means change in form or appearance.

Such has been my case for two years. After filing for a divorce almost nine years ago, I feared the unknown; could I make it on my own by myself and what would be my destiny in this life? God blessed us with six wonderful children to bring to this earth, which seemed our only purpose. My ex-husband never wanted me to have a career in fashion, which was my background. Once I said "I do," he said I didn't have to work. Many times I would get a part-time job and when he would comment that I love my job more than him, I would quit. When we met I had just completed a degree in fashion merchandising. My dreams in my youth were to work in retail, the creative part of all of it, designing and creating. That ending of my life opened up a brand-new path for me to walk down. Many times in our lives we think of an ending as the end of our journey, which turns out to be the beginning of another purpose-filled journey. The Bible clearly states, *"Don't be conformed to this world (earthly/human ways), but be ye transformed (remade, reborn, renew; re- means to do over again) by the renewal of your mind (Spirit ways), so that you (YOU) may prove what is the good and acceptable and perfect will of God, even the thing which is good and acceptable and perfect"* (Romans 12:2). When I pondered the text from the Bible and how it applied in my life, I followed the conforms of this world.

Often I thought others, well-meaning people, knew more than I did. I didn't completely trust my gut reactions. I lacked faith and confidence in my own decisions. Not until I decided to change my thoughts, to get healthy again, and to renew my personal core values of what I wanted in life did I begin to become renewed. Many people have asked me how I became transformed, and this is why I am writing to you, the reader who wants to make a spirit, body, soul, and mind transformation. As you read and digest the material contained here, many lack the courage and discipline to achieve a personal transformation; others may have high demands on their personal and family lives that can be assessed only by them; or fear comes into play which has to be acknowledged and removed only by them. Which one of the examples applies to your reasoning? This title is very appropriate, *In Due Season: Destiny is Calling Your Soul*, because in reality Destiny is always calling us to some work if we would just listen -- and answer the call to service, whatever it may be. You are the co-designer in your life's journey. Start building. Take an inventory of your gifts, talents, abilities, strengths, and weaknesses.

My soul became renewed as I continually tried to lose weight, get healthy, remember my buried dreams from childhood, and find my purpose. Now, I thought, I must face my inner demons to truly transform myself at age 49 for 50. Before the age of 40, I was healthy and only ate nutritional foods for my body. I had already changed my diet to a healthier one at age 26. Our family has a long history of cancer. Since I was five years old, I can remember my grandmother's death of colon cancer and the rest of the family. I did not want to face this disease. I gained 20 pounds the first two years after my divorce. I wore size 10 clothing. The 3rd and 4th years I wore a size 12 and stayed there until 2005. The unmanaged stress, meeting my financial obligations and the challenges of the divorce, and raising five children on my own left me vulnerable and unhealthy in body and spirit. As a woman over the age of 40, I built up a huge amount of stress hormones.

In 2004, weighing 184 pounds, and having a body mass index (BMI) of 35, I was certainly not in good health. This was not good for the heart of a woman over 40. I began getting ready for my 50th birthday and my new image. I had been pretty ill with a condition called fibromyalgia (muscle pain/autoimmune deficiency) and ragweed allergies. Being sick didn't keep me from lifting my table to go to work, but limited me on some days with muscle pain, stiffness, itchy eyes, stuff y nose, congestion, and very low spirits.

I asked myself, could I really be transformed? How long will it take? I knew that anything worth it is never easy. I joined the YMCA across the street from my home and sought natural and medical treatment for my conditions. Here I am applying my faith right into action. At this point I got up early and prepared to leave my home to head out to the YMCA. The first month I did kickboxing two days a week and yoga once a week. I started off slowly.

The questions still came about from what I had been told or learned about fibromyalgia. Doctors told me that I couldn't do major exercises like high-impact aerobics. The physical demands of aerobic exercise increase the body's consumption of oxygen and improve the functioning of the circulatory system. A year before I was diagnosed with sleep apnea, and I had to use a breathing machine to get oxygen at night.

Losing weight has enhanced my sleep, but my tongue is too big for my throat area.

Kickboxing became my best friend twice a week. Kickboxing challenged me to push my muscles where they hadn't been. With a daily dose of spiritual practices, discipline, courage, and confidence I was able to get moving. I felt energized! My goal was to build six-pack abs. Are you ready for some discipline in your life? I sure was.

I started using Epsom salts for my sore muscles drank fresh juice daily made from carrots, ginger, spinach, celery, and garlic, along with three cups of detox herbal tea. I stopped eating all sugars, red meats, and pork. Next, I sought out a low-carbohydrate diet (only 40 grams of carbs a day) and eliminated breads. My body, my mental outlook, and my health started changing in appearance and endurance. I still wore a size 12 for six more months, though, as my abs were still big. I increased my kickboxing to three days a week, and switched from yoga to Pilates, three days a week, to strengthen my abs.

Change was happening now. Within three months I was wearing a size 8. With the muscle stiffness associated with the disease,

I learned to do low-impact exercises, such as biking, swimming, and water aerobics. I was determined to overcome this weakness and determination became my daily mantra. *Determination* means to decide with one's mind firmly made up, focused, on a purpose or a goal. In my mind I visualized myself doing all aerobics, even high impact, slowly, a month at a time. Visualization is vitally important to reaching your personal goals. This was going on within my spirit down deep inside. A voice was saying, "Carol you can do it, you can master this goal. You will win over your weakness."

Twenty-one years of marriage and four Caesarean births (including 7-lb. twins), had stretched my abdominal muscles beyond imagination. *To fortify* means that when we build ourselves up with added foods rich in vitamins, herbs, and minerals in our daily foods, we have enriched our body to function well.

Take a moment and look on the ingredients on the box of your favorite cereals. Do you understand enrichment and fortify now? A bath consisting of two cups of Epsom salts along with ½ cup of baking soda, ½ cup of sea salt with three tablets of vitamin C relaxed my muscles and removed the lactic acid. Topically, lactic acid makes the skin smooth by removing dead skin. Internally, it causes discomfort before or after exercise. Drinking natural apple cider vinegar with eight ounces of water three times a day helped to remove the lactic acid, reduced my sinus problems, and flushed my kidneys. Apple skins contain malic acid, which is necessary for attacking lactic acid within the body. Vitamin B 100s helped me become balanced within my nerves, muscles, and cells. The B6 vitamins helped with muscle pain. Hyaluronic acid, another supplement, helps to support soft tissue in the muscles as well as the skin. MSM and glucosamine, two major components that repair damaged cartilage in the bones as a result of weight loss, both tighten the skin. Of course, calcium, magnesium, zinc and, again, vitamin C were also used at night to replenish my bones, nerves, tendons, blood, and muscles. Calcium leaks out at night, so it really should be taken at night for best results.

Remember that I am a massage therapist, which is hard work with a bad back in the lumbar area, muscle aches and pains, and faced with fibromyalgia. I used one dropper of liquid yucca, an herb used for inflammation of the joints and pain.

Initially, I added yoga once a week to reduce the strains of my hectic life that left me with physical pain and disease. My emotions and mental outlook were unbalanced as well. I had held onto childhood, adulthood, and physical pain and suffering within my body, which stored these in my cell memory. B.K.S. Iyengar, the renowned yoga practitioner, has taught yoga for sixty years and believes that yoga integrates the mental and the physical plane, offering a sense of inner and outer balance or alignment. True alignment means that the inner mind reaches every cell and fiber of the body. Yoga is an ancient science of one's body, mind, and soul. It calmed my impulses and stressful lifestyle. Many religious people in the West are afraid of the yoga/meditation practice even though doctors are finding out through study about how the mind/body practice helps assist healing within the body. According to the Buddhist point of view, meditation develops a discipline that creates a spiritual path. It allows one to have a form of control over actions, negative thoughts, and emotions. In order to lose weight and change to a healthier lifestyle, we must gain control over our physical, emotional, mental, and negative thought patterns. It has been proven that when trying to eliminate a negative behavior, one must replace it with positive actions for at least 30 days. This can only be done one day at a time. I had to retrain my mind to love, and to convince myself to get out of bed and eliminate the excess baggage of negative emotions and fat cells.

Next, I had to remove the distractions that were making me focus my energy somewhere else. A few of those distractions included clutter in my soul, home, and people, places, and things that no longer served me. A spiritual practice helped me to focus on the successful goals. As I said before, my spiritual practice was prayer, meditation, visualization, listening while being still, working out at home or the gym, and faith in myself along with faith in God.

So often we are too busy doing this or that, going here or there. How often do you take the chance to sit and ponder, to reach deep within for an answer? Do you really understand and know how to apply the principles of letting go or surrendering? As I used prayer, fasting, meditation, and listening I was able to give up to the powers of my sacred source, surrender, and let go. Matthew 4:2 shows how Jesus gained

strength to overcome the temptations of eating or giving away His powers by fasting for 40 days and nights. Various Eastern and Western religions fast along with using prayer to reconnect, to gain strength, to create a newness within, and to let go of old ways (shedding), purifying their body temples. Just like the Master teacher Jesus, who set a perfect example on how to overcome weakness within our souls, the followers and believers
of the Church of Jesus Christ of Latter Day Saints fast once a month as a church body to show compassion and empathy to those who are in need of shelter, food, and love within their church body. Th ey refrain from two meals a day on the first Sunday of the month and donate that
money to the church for the needy. An Eastern religion, the Baha' faith, related to the Middle Eastern and Asian culture and religions have similar symbolic relations. They often fast during the year; however in the springtime they fast the entire month of March from sunrise to sundown, always ending their fast with a celebration of food, music, and happiness called a feast.

A long time friend of mine, a massage therapist who happens to be blind, practices Buddhism. She was raised in a traditional religious setting. As a baby she often suffered abuse at the hands of her mother. I talked with her about her newfound spiritual practice of Buddhism. This ancient practice has helped her break free from her troubled childhood pain. When she arises in the morning, she sits in silence and chants, listening to the still small voice within her soul. Afterward she does her morning yoga. This friend tends to suffer with some affrications within her structure (bones) that yoga alleviates. In the past she suffered from panic attacks, but she has not had any more since she discovered a spiritual practice that is right for her. She listens to tapes from the monks and other inspiring spiritual teachers such as Ester Hicks. She has gained wholeness in her soul, which she had previously lacked for many years before now. Learning to break old habits and replace them with new ones has excited her. She is aware of how she copes now; she doesn't see things in black and white, or good or bad. It's all her choice on how she perceives things going on in her life. She is in charge of her own destiny for once. Her blindness has nothing to do with her soul's progression in this lifetime; she doesn't see blindness as a weakness the way like she did many years before. She's no longer a victim. She said it's all in how she wants to believe it and see it. No longer is bitterness, sadness, or anger a part of her life. She has learned compassion for her mother and her father, who didn't protect her from the abuse. She is not dating right now, in order to heal – to forgive completely, and move on (surrender) so she may have a healthy relationship with someone one day. In her own words she says, "I now trust the universe in all things, knowing that all things in my life are already perfect and so am I." Stepping out from the norm of her family's beliefs was hard for her, but on the other hand she must be praised for doing what is right for her soul's spiritual practice.

Yogic science finds that there are five basic states of mind. These states of mind are lethargic, distracted, scattered, focused, and controlled. In other words, when I was unable to concentrate when reading, talking, or listening to others and needed to prioritize my time or goals, yoga transformed me in the following ways: combating failure, changing from helplessness to calmness, developing the ability to tell the difference between true and false realities in my perceived problems, and bringing back a scattered mind.

My traumatic divorce and lifestyle had left me facing many obstacles, and it appeared that my personal goals were unattainable. I have learned, as my massage therapist friend did, that there are many things we can gain when facing obstacles if only we would learn to embrace them instead of resisting them. Now my life had a true purpose; doubt and fear started to leave me a little more each day.

Confidence, positive self-talk, and a new attitude became my discipline. I had to quiet the inner negative voices with my spirit and the negative voices of others from the past. Next I created a new avenue for me to master my goals. Then I worked on the positive voices from other sources within and help that were sent to me by Spirit. Do you understand how to use meditation? The Psalms of the Holy Scriptures were written to teach us that God has a personal concern for all of us. Again God allows us freedom to choose. As long as we are alive, there will be so called difficulties we must face; therefore, seeking God's direction through mediation and prayer is necessary. This is our time to seek God's face and God's answers. Psalm 1:2 states, "But his delight (God) is the law of

the lord; and his law doth he meditate day and night." Prayer is an
open communication between you and your sacred source. Psalm 10:17, *"The Lord has heard the desire of the humble; thou will cause thine ear to hear."* In order to hear, the ego of self must be gone; humbleness produces humility. The Spirit's prompting will come into your ears when you are humble and let go of the need to have an ego. You then will have directions, inspiration, and clarity in all things you need in time. For an example: You may want to lose five more pounds and you may not think this is important to Spirit. Try the above instructions; trust and see whatever you need if an answer is not given in time.

At this point I want to introduce some key words that became important to my *healthy lifestyle transformation.* Determination is necessary to understand and hold onto if you want change within yourself. When faced with stressful outcomes and confusion on the daily journey, one must decide or be determined to become stronger, to gain maturity within oneself and the Spirit of the universe.

Perceptions of unhappiness, fatigue, and confusion are not always what the mind

leads you to believe under stress.
Determination becomes a good habit to
develop in order to achieve a very important
goal. Spiritual practice, yoga, kickboxing,
and my supplements allowed me to gain
mind over matter, to let go, and to see events
for what they really were at this time. A few
have asked me how they can learn to let go.
Most of us on this planet have unknowingly
carried more on our shoulders than is
required of us, which has caused us to
become codependent; I have been
for over 40 years. Finally I learned through
trial and error and daily living what is mine
and what is yours, and I left yours alone. On
this journey of personal transformation I've
learned that I needed to love me, to honor
me, and to care for me during my own
recovery for me; no one else
was going to do it. I encouraged myself and
supported myself without any guilt or
shame. So when faced with what appeared
to be negative situations or trials, if I could
help prevent it, I did.

There is growth in all things. If I could redo
over another way I did. If the problem
wasn't
fixable by me I put it into my sacred
source's hands and left it there. I didn't go
back to pick it up again. My eyes were not

fixed on the problem again. Surrender, Let Go, and Let God became my motto and I gave thanks to God because it was already perfect, just as my friend had said. Releasing the person, place, or thing into the air, up, up and away it went. The next thing I knew, the problem was fixed. Then I again gave thanks and appreciation to God.

The next word is *fortitude:* strength against attack, support; *fortify:* strengthening, enriching with vitamins/minerals protecting the body from harm. In Latin it means strength, patience, courage facing pain. Whenever you start a new regimen, your mind/body comes under attack. The mind is actually in the body and exists all over.

It has been said by B.K.S. Iyengar that the mind can be a secret enemy and a treacherous friend. It can influence our behavior before we have time to consider causes and consequences. My healthy meals, meditation and prayers, juices, herbs, teas, vitamins, and minerals helped fortify my journey so that my mind would influence me and my body for good. Well-meaning friends and family members have good intentions; however, it may appear that they discourage you from reaching your goals because they don't fully understand the mission, purpose, and path of your journey. It's best to keep your heart's desires, wishes, and your newfound journey private and away from others.

Others often try to make us conform to their will, partly because they are unsure of what they want for themselves. You must understand clearly what it is you are reaching to achieve and be secure within that knowledge. For me, I kept it between me and the God I serve. This is the Law of Attraction; at the time I was doing this process I didn't know it had a name. You can be healthier, I can do all things I want to do, and you and I both can have everything we
want in this lifetime. I told three people that I knew held me to their highest good for my life. They prayed for me and supported me. Others noticed my transformation and wanted to know what I had done. Manifesting is the results of living the Laws of Attraction. I only told a small portion of the transformation journey because it was still being tested daily.

The other word to truly understand is *resilience*. I was doing spinning and yoga when this word flooded into my spirit along with fortitude. I came home and looked all of them up in my dictionary. The power to spring back, quality in nature, elasticity like in rubber is the definition of resilience. The dictionary went on to express the power of recovering after being stretched, a resilient nature that knows of trouble. When you desire a certain outcome in your life, you face seen and unseen problems or obstacles and you can become distracted from your journey and lose your clarity and stability. Many times the advice that people offer withdraws, and you spring back like elastic that's been stretched beyond its means. A friend once told me of her experience during a hurricane. After the storm, she noticed that the palm trees had made it through, whereas the bigger and stronger-seeming trees had fallen over. The resilience of the palms allowed them to give into the wind without snapping, but the bigger trees had no elasticity or flexibility, so they broke and fell over. While trying to get my transformation I was stretched over and over; I know what I am made up of. We should approach our destiny like the palm— no snapping, just gaining flexibility and elasticity enough to bend over and over again till we reach our goals.

To achieve any transformation for a goal you must become disciplined, yet resilient, in your everyday life. Negative thoughts by you and others rebuke your experience. At this point mind renewal is a must. You can't afford to go back to the old ways of thinking and acting, or you will lose sight of your new goals. Surround yourself only with positive, uplifting experiences to help you in the facets of everyday life. A consciousness of truth in your mind, a fasting spirit, prayer, meditation, and body help you to make open choices in your situations. You are free to choose life or death or to become detained on your journey. Which one will you choose? A positive attitude, a supportive network of people, knowing your intentions, unclouding your mind and intellect, thinking to achieve the next level on your journey – all of these are needed.

As a human, spiritual being you are faced daily with uncontrollable situations and you must spring back without losing your center (no distractions) within your heart, soul, and spirit. If your belief system is spiritual, trust the God of the Universe, your Sacred Source, Jesus Christ, Buddha, Mohammed, or whatever your religious belief system is; it's your choice. But most of all trust yourself; trust that you have the ability to be liberated from the negative path you've taken. There are many roads and paths to travel to achieve wholeness to a healthier lifestyle of transformation and purpose. The end results are too many to list. Mine were achieved by having a desire, discipline, trusting in my God, trusting in myself, learning not to hold onto what wasn't mine and letting go of what was too much for me to handle, and concentration. The blessings are many: self-awareness, truth of what I have become, peace, and an understanding of tranquility. But I had to surrender and detach myself from the outcome of my desired results, let go, and trust the process and my God. So when you get off -focus on your journey -- and you will, spin back, reorganize, start over, forgive yourself for not achieving what you wanted, forgive God for the times you thought Spirit wasn't there helping, and forgive others for not helping you achieve your desired goal as expected.

Or just maybe you felt they interrupted your focus; it was yours to do alone. When you choose to surrender to what comes your way, you must know that your actions are correct. When one door closes, many open to you. You must believe in your purpose and plan of action. Never lose sight of your big picture; it is yours and yours alone.

There will be many roadblocks, stop lights, detours, and bad storms from the weather; just go with the flow of life, learn to let go, and trust God. Now do you know how to "let go and let God" work in your life? If so write it here: As we move on to another level of understanding, let's journey into a beginning of a *healthy lifestyle transformation.*

1. Understand your purpose and determination:

       • Ask yourself, what is your desired transformation outcome and write it here?

       • Example: I want to become healthy, no more sugar. In two years I want to travel across the ocean.

       • No one knows the answers but you; it's yours alone to look and listen within your soul. An affirmation: I will not touch sugar. To receive your answer you must be open! Go within to get your truth and answers.

              • Example: I will watch the amount of grams of sugar in everything I eat for three months. Sugar makes me sad afterwards.

• Write your goals in a journal, and clarify what you want to achieve. Ask every morning "How my I serve?"

• Example: October 11, Monday: I want to be a size 14 by July 4, my birthday! My goal will be to walk every day for an hour.

2. Pray, Forgive, Visualize, Meditate, Believe in your Transformation. Focus on your breath when meditating. While meditating if thoughts come into your mind just let them fl oat away into nothing. Light a scented candle if you can handle the scents. I focus on the flame burning with my eyes opened. Then I internalize that flame burning within my soul, bringing everything I need to me for my good and burning away anything I don't need. Transformation will leave you fatigued or energized. How you feel will be determined by your perception and the message you send your body/ mind connection. In the order of your day *develop awareness* of your achievements and what's needed to complete your daily goals. Remember the goals are to become transformed, not conformed, by the renewing of the mind.

• Ask, seek, knock, and then open the door for fast results. Help is available to you through Spirit -- just ask; it is very simple. Guide me, direct my pathways, and open new ways that I can create what I need on my transformation. I thank you, Spirit.

3. Balance: another word that could be used is harmony. We are spiritual beings on this earth in a human body. To face your inner demons and start your transformation, find a supportive outlet or person. Everyone needs someone who will hold him or her accountable. Take the "one day at a time" approach to help you maintain your focus and balance. For me it was the instructors at the YMCA and a few close friends. Everyone needs or has a social outlet and positive setting that is spiritually uplifting and creates a physical balance, called playtime. Many do yoga to improve their balance in their bodies and life.

4. Do you have *me* time to be alone with yourself? Use resilience (spring back) daily to help balance your new healthy lifestyle journey. Do you love you?

5. Learn to become proactive and take risks. Do you put limitations on you and God on improving your transformation? Step out in faith and exercise in faith that you will become transformed. Believe that you have already achieved your outcomes. Get out of the comforts of your life. Try a new exercise class or a new salad. Explore other creative ways to achieve your personal goals. Only you and God understand what it is that you need. You will be sent all information needed to you by others; you will receive the help only if your heart is open. Think outside and around the box. It has been stated that when the teacher is ready the student will show up. We all take on different roles from time to time; be a lifelong learner.

6. Letting go of controlling the desired outcome is what gives you the opportunity for your growth. This much needed process doesn't take place only in a physical form, but in emotional, mental, human, and spiritual forms for your well being. So often we want to have a fast weight loss so others and the ego can see it instantly. We should focus on shedding the negative emotions, false illusions, and excess baggage from many trips in our mind, body, spirit, hurts, disappointments, sadness, fears, guilt, and

more. Just like we clean out drawers, closets, and bathrooms, we must clean out the attic of our minds, free the clutter, forgive God, others, and ourselves for our mistakes, and renew our spirits. Let go of old concepts that are no longer of any use. You will learn or be given by Spirit new ones if you let go of the old ones. Let go of people, places, and things that don't hold you in great esteem. Let go of your need to control everyone and everything or to fix every problem. Surrender means to give up to the possession or power of another. Be at peace. Detox your emotions and you will be amazed that your spirit will be so light and full of love. As I approached my transformation I made a huge change, leaving all things behind and embracing a new future. T e Bible says, *"Now faith is the substance of things hoped for, the evidence of things not seen"* (Hebrews 11:1, KJV). My personal transformation was a hope that I wanted, yet it was unseen until later. Are you willing to put your faith into action today? Here are two quotes I leave you on faith. Bertrand Russell says, "To conquer fear is the beginning of wisdom."

Next, "Faith is our direct link to universal wisdom, reminding us that we know more than
we have only to look, listen, and trust the love and wisdom of the Universal Spirit working through us all," from the book *The Laws of Spirit,* by Dan Millman. I ask you, what are the fears that you need to conquer in order to realize your wisdom through faith?

Chapter 2
Transformation in Progress: Hard Work Pays Off

"Victory is not won in miles, but in inches."
—Louis L'Amour

After 4 months of hard work and labor, finally something was changing or transforming me! My weight loss was now 10 pounds; my legs were slimming down and starting to shape and tone well; however, my belly was still the same. Daily I discovered a new endurance and stamina. Muscular stiffness from the fibromyalgia was still there, but mind-over-matter began a needed head trip. Bath salts were extremely necessary to accomplish the next day's workout plan.

After 40, women's metabolism slows down. Dr. Don Colbert, author of *The Bible Cure*, states that an overconsumption of carbohydrates, starches, and sugars stimulates your body's production of insulin—the body's fat storage hormone. Insulin lowers blood sugar levels; when they are too high they cause the body to store fat. This was my problem. I craved carbohydrates when I was bored, stressed, or tired. If I continued to eat carbohydrates, my

insulin levels would stay high and fat would be stored into my cells. Changing my diet to a healthy one was the only answer if I wanted to lose abdominal fat. Bloating, gas, and indigestion decreased once I limited my sweets, i.e., cookies, fruit drinks, soft drinks, pastries, candies, etc.
(Some foods that are also high in carbohydrates are rice, corn, potatoes, pasta, and breads.)

According to Colbert, it is then changed into blood sugar. In the presence of insulin, the blood sugar is converted into blood fat by the liver. The fat in the blood is then stored away into the fat
cells. (Detox tea with dandelion as well as milk thistle in a capsule or liquid tincture is helpful for cleansing and rebuilding the liver. Milk thistle, however, loses its potency when made into a tea and must not be mixed in water for a tea.)

Do you know the abdominal muscles? The transverse abdominals (lower abs) run across (think girdle). The transverse abdominals' function is to compress the abdomen, keeping everything in place. Once I increased my fiber, this went down! The rectus abdominus, the sixpack muscle, helps your upper body to bend (to crunch). I had to strengthen my rectus abdominus to get my posture corrected. Pilates and yoga helped me with this mission.

My biggest problem was the obliques. External obliques go down the sides of your waist starting at the ribs. They hung over my pants. The internal obliques are between the ribcage and the external obliques run down the sides of your body. I strengthened these muscles and now I breathe better, even though I have seasonal allergies!

Since I was told to do Pilates to strengthen my core muscles, I asked what these were and why I should strengthen them. Joseph Pilates developed the Pilates method, which encourages the isolation of muscles or muscle groups, requiring mental attention. The core muscles are between the shoulder and hip bones. This includes the back muscles. If you strengthen the abs, you strengthen glutes, back muscles, and leg muscles as well.

My back pain in the lumbar area was related to the weak muscles in my mid-section near the heart. More women die yearly from heart attacks. The editor-in-chief of *Men's Health* stated that the arteries in the lower body constrict while the heart dramatically increases output. He also mentioned that with extra padding around your gut, your heart pumps harder to force blood into all that new fatty tissue. When you line your arteries with plaque from too many fatty meals, blood pressure increases because the same amount of blood has to squeeze through the newly narrowed vessels. (I know this is a lot of information, but it is important for you to understand why women over 40 have big bellies.) He goes on to say that as the pressures of the day haunt you into the night, your brain pumps out stress hormones that keep your body in a perpetual state of fight or flight, forcing the heart to pump harder. My new daily routine would be (this may not be necessarily the best one for you):

• 5 AM – Take two Hoodia diet supplements with eight ounces of water with lemon juice, cayenne pepper, or apple cider vinegar upon waking, along with one tablespoon of flaxseed oil. (Omega-3s rebalance fatty acids, lower cholesterol, reduce the risk of heart disease, relieve irritable bowel syndrome associated with fibromyalgia, and much more.) Lemon juice stimulates the liver; cider vinegar curbs food cravings; and cayenne pepper stimulates the colon, kidneys, and liver. Then I go to the gym for

45 minutes of spin, weights, or kickboxing. This exercise is done three times a week. I am self-employed, which allows me more fl ex time.

• 6 AM - Drink one cup of detox tea (no honey or sugar) and do 30 minutes of yoga and meditation, along with prayer.

• 7 AM – ½ cup low fat soy milk with low sugar cereal (110 calories), vitamins (water in between).

• 8:15 AM – Kickboxing three days a week

• 9 AM – eight ounces of fresh vegetable juice and ten almonds, pecans, or walnuts.

• 12 noon – Take two Hoodia diet supplements; fish, chicken; or turkey, vegetables— fresh or
frozen, salad (vitamins), eight ounces of water, and herbal tea.

• Naptime between 1 p.m. and 2 p.m.

• 3 PM – Nuts, low-fat yogurt with low or no sugar, apple or pear, eight ounces of water, Pilates for one hour three days a week.

• 4 PM – Herbal tea, eight ounces of water.

• 5 PM – Take two Hoodia diet supplements; vegetables, lean meat, eight ounces of water with lemon or apple cider vinegar.

• 7 PM – Protein snack, no or low sugar, low-fat soy smoothie or yogurt, nuts or boiled egg whites, peanut or almond butter, eight ounces of water, warm herbal tea, one tablespoon of flaxseed oil.

Sometimes I wanted another heavy starch snack. I fixed popcorn in coconut oil on my stove. Then I added parsley, garlic, lemon/pepper salt, and red pepper. I ate two to three cups and also added almonds. Another snack I enjoyed was carob-covered almonds from Wild Oats Market; carob is a chocolate substitute.

There were certain supplements that I took daily. One of them was Hoodia, an herb from Africa that suppresses the appetite. I took six a day, to complete 1000 mg. To reduce my stress and belly fat and to support my metabolism, I took Cortislim supplements. This formula states that it maintains healthy blood sugar levels. Its ingredients are:

Green tea extract – helps metabolism

Chromium – supports blood sugar

Guarana seed – mental alertness

Glucomannan blend – healthy blood sugar

Vitamins B6 and B12 – helps convert stored
carbohydrates to energy and supports
healthy red
blood cells.

Niacin – converts food to energy.

Vitamin B 100 mg, three times a day

Vitamin C 500 mg, three times a day

Chromium 500 mg, three times a day

Magnesium 500 mg, three times a day

MSM & Glucosamine 870 mg, two times a
day

Hyaluronic Acid 20 mg, three times a day

Gingko Bilboa, 500 mg, two times a day

Women's daily multivitamin, once a day

Flaxseed oil, two tablespoons daily

At night before bed, Calcium 1000 mg,
Magnesium 600 mg, and Zinc 15 mg all
together.

Herbal teas – Detox with dandelion for liver
support and kidney function. I drank this tea
before 5 p.m. at night.

Green tea with Echinacea for immune
support. I drink Echinacea tea every other
month only.

Chamomile tea before retiring.

*Always check with your healthcare
provider before going on any new diet or
exercise plan to make sure that what you
chose is the best for your body. There are
magazines/DVDs/tapes for yoga and abs
exercises with examples you could benefit
from at your local book store. You may
want to check your local library (free) and
online for additional information.

I recommend the book *The Abs Diet* by
David Zinczenko. It's a six-week plan to
flatten your stomach and keep you lean for

life. Once I was told about Pilates, I chose to do it. I didn't like the challenging and hard exercises, but once I saw my belly lengthen and tone, I committed myself to three times a week. I also had to cut back on alcohol because it produces sugar and dehydrates the body, skin, and other organs. I didn't use caffeine, so coffee was never a problem for me; however, it can cause the same problems as alcohol.

We started off in the roll downs. For the first nine months, I could not hold the pose down, but once I conquered the most important move—the navel to spine, I performed it every day while kickboxing, walking, cleaning my home, or driving. Within nine months my abdominals were shrinking. Oftentimes during Pilates we used the balls, bands, or weights. I had three different teachers who taught their own separate ways. Here are a few moves:

• The **side jackknife** targets the obliques. We lie on the floor on our right or left hips and raise our torsos off the floor with forearms on the floor for balance. The other hand is placed behind the ear with the elbow pointed toward the feet. We lift our legs toward the torso while keeping the rest of the body still. Ten repetitions were done on each side.

• For the transverse abdominals, one teacher made us hold **plank** forever! We started in a pushup
position, on the elbow, and rested with weights on forearms. With the body in a straight line, our feet were over our toes. We did five repetitions.

• **Single knee crunch**, oh me! They all said at the YMCA that it focuses on upper and lower abs
as we lie on our backs with hips bent and feet on the floor. Fingers on the sides of the head, elbows bent, touching at the knee, we did 10 repetitions.

So you get the idea. All the while we are doing the hour of Pilates the navel is pulled to the spine, with shoulders and neck lifted. Within twelve months of the abs reconstruction, I became fl at. The hardest challenge was my over-sized obliques. This was a major problem.

Strong abdominals stabilize and support your entire body. They also help your body to move better. Then I bought Sublime Slimgel by L'Oreal at the drugstore. It targets abs by tightening and toning; my stomach liked this product because it became firmer and flatter.

In the year of my 50th birthday I was losing breast tissue; my abdominals were shrinking; and my legs and thighs were beautiful. I had energy and my allergies were healed.

It was fall, which was my usual time for ragweed pollen allergies. It was a breeze. My weight was 160 pounds now! Although I was at a size 8, my arms were not toned. Now it was time to do machines to tone my pectoral muscles, triceps, and biceps for my breasts and arms. Did you realize that we have over 20 different muscles in our arms? I am only going to mention three: biceps, the top front of your extended arm; triceps, the back and bottom of your extended arm; and deltoids, in your upper shoulder and arm. The benefits from upper body machines allowed me to pop up my muscle in my biceps. When doing kickboxing, we make a "hook" movement
with the biceps that allows the elbow to bend. We push an extended movement or pound our fi st. In Pilates or yoga we do pushups or push away. In kickboxing, or Tae-Bo, Billy Blanks says the triceps is the

muscle that delivers the punch. When I would hit the bags during kickboxing, the teachers would have me move my arms forward, back, down or up, even over. The muscle used is the deltoid.

To build my breasts, as I stated before, I turned to machines and weights. I was afraid of those machines. One year later though, my chest (pectoralis major and pectoralis minor) was being built up. Little did I know how they worked! I am sure I had learned in massage school but that was years ago, so I did some research. The pectorals are pushing muscles. The minor brings your shoulder forward and downward. Pushups are recommended for building them. When the kickboxing bag is hit, the chest muscle delivers the punch, and the latissimus dorsi pulls it back! As I mention the latissimus dorsi, this is my latest target muscle, along with the stubborn obliques. I do 50 to 65 pounds of upper body machine, three sets of ten, three times a week (every other day).

One year later I am now doing kickboxing three times a week, upper body machines, Pilates three times a week, yoga every morning at home for thirty minutes, and spinning 4 days a week.

My heart rate is 70% to 80%! Exercises tone, firm, and build muscles. I needed to lose calories and strengthen my heart; so raising my heart rate was necessary in the spinning or kickboxing classes. My arms, shoulders, and chest are now toned and looking sexy and beautiful. Many people ask me if I lift weights!

On my birthday, people came in looking at me and saying I should model. I had just seen a national model search for women over 40 and fabulous. Then I remembered when I was 12, looking at *Seventeen* magazine and thinking that I should be in the magazine. At 14 I entered my first national model search for *Seventeen* magazine and became a finalist! It's funny how your brain blocks out these things of importance to you. This was my passion and my dream, to model. So at this point, I called *More* magazine to see when their next search was and was to be held in 2006 with winners announced in 2007.

As this chapter ends, get your fitness, spiritual, mental, and emotional goals set. Never lose sight! If you do, just return slowly. I did! Dare to dream your aspirations and dreams that have been within your soul for years. I found this quote, which I leave for you to meditate on:

"Far away, there in the sunshine, are my highest aspirations. I may not reach them, but I can look up and see their beauty, believe in them, and try to follow where they lead." (Unknown Author)

"Group fitness classes are a great way for people of all ages and capabilities to get motivated, meet others with similar goals, and be held accountable. Indoor cycling classes are done on a stationary bike and led by a certified instructor who starts with a proper warmup, a simulated course, and a cool down; all of which are set to motivating music. Pilates classes typically consist of mat exercises that are designed to strengthen and stretch the core muscles of the body. Yoga uses traditional body poses to connect mind, body, and spirit. Originally, Yoga was practiced to meditate, pray, heal, and restore energy." Helen Shivak. National Strength and Conditioning Association Certified Personal Trainer (NSCA-CPT), Aerobics and Fitness Association of America (AFAA) certified personal trainer and group fitness, PiYo certified
through Powder Blue Productions etc.

Chapter 3
Get Ready, My Soul

Get ready my soul
I'm diving in
Get ready my soul
I'm diving in
To the deepest kind of love
To the sweetest kind of life
Get ready my soul
Get ready my soul.
Everything I've ever done
Everything I've ever seen
Everything I've ever lost or won
Everything I've ever dreamed.
Here I go
Deeper, deeper,
Deeper than I've ever been before.
Here I go
Closer to my sacred source.
—Daniel Nahmod

What is your *sacred source*? Do you have a relationship with your source? Do you have a sacred source place within your home? If you don't know, this may be a good time for you to examine it in your life. Within the Silence and listening you may find your source. I have learned to appreciate the gift of the Silence. Fear and critical self-talk have been two of the deepest negative emotions that I've had to overcome. For me negative self-talk was learned, as stated before. Then I believed it for many years thereafter; consequently, transforming my mindset was extremely necessary. This reminded me of the 3rd principle of Unity in Chapter 1; review it, please.

Another setback was procrastination, or fear to start—I just had to stop putting off everything I needed to do. An inspiring quote from motivational speaker Dale Carnegie, says, "If you want to conquer fear, don't sit at home and think about it. Go out and get busy."

Fear senses can be your protector, says Dr. Viscott in his book *Emotional Resilience*. In it he speaks of fear. He says, in essence, that if you had no fear you would have been dead long ago. When anxious, you feel that something is wrong. It's your job to understand why you feel the way you do. Anxiety can also lead you to misinterpret what you perceive. Learn to see fear as a weakness, and then gain faith. Confidence is your belief that you will survive being afraid. Most people use fear as a weakness to do nothing. Once I realized that I could do all things with a firm belief in my Higher Power, in God, one step at a time transformation unfolded daily. Like in the words of the song, my soul got ready.

What's keeping you from reaching your goals?

I openly admitted to myself and to others my thoughts on why I couldn't lose weight. It was my view; however, my view was not correct. The fear was that I couldn't do cardio exercises because of the fibromyalgia might be true for another, but boy, was I wrong as far as I'm concerned! I went slowly at first and added more exercises as my muscles retrained; I challenged myself and got stronger.

My fear could have left the weight on my body and the pain in my soul, but all that is now removed. I pushed the limits within my soul and it worked. Oftentimes we put too many limits and lack trust in our God by leaving the Spirit out of our decisions. We limit ourselves because of the negative thoughts about ourselves that we have carried for years. Not only that, but how many times have we limited our family members and friends out of our own fears, doubt, jealousy, or pain?

Have you admitted your past failures, lack of courage and deep-seated fears? List them here.

1.
2.
3.
4.
5.

Create Plans for Action

I woke up one day and became proactive and took a personal responsibility for my soul's recovery. I had to take personal responsibility and look within honestly. I suffered emotionally, physically, mentally, and spiritually, and I desperately wanted a personal transformation. Suddenly committed, I decided to get up and get out the door and to the gym to make a difference. Keeping a daily fitness journal to chart my progress and emotions enabled me to

express my feelings more clearly. I can't tell you too often about how you should keep this personal transformation between yourself and your God and just a few friends. The

energy loses strength when you share with everyone what you trying to see happen.

There is a time to share, but not when at the beginning. Through prayer, meditation, willingness, visualization, and being proactive, I was able to get up and walk through the doors for my desired results.

What are your courageous new plans for action? List them here.

1.
2.
3.
4.
5.

The veteran actress Mary Tyler Moore stated, "Take chances, make mistakes. That's how you grow. Pain nourishes your courage. You have to fail in order to practice being brave."

With no excuses and no regrets, getting my soul ready daily slowly improved my confidence. The old negative thought patterns were gone. Reread the lyrics of the song at the beginning of this chapter. Sit and meditate. Ponder its meaning. As I opened up to creative new energies and invited the universal God to recreate newness within my soul, I was now in a co-partnership with God. Have you ever been fearful about starting over? It's all a trick of your mind. Just start over and forgive yourself for your supposed distractions. It's okay. The challenge is not with someone else. You are competing with and comparing yourself to others. Focus on your challenge. Take your eyes and focus off the others in your path. Find your sacred source and create your space within your own soul and home. Start celebrating the newness of you.

Do you fear working out and just being alone? You are never alone. Acknowledge your sacred source, your Higher Power, and ask for guidance to complete your task. Many fear being alone because it's then that negative feelings creep into their souls. Others like affirmations from others that they are on the right and purposeful path.

Speak positive words of encouragement and affirmations to yourself in order to achieve your desired outcome. Learn to listen to the still, small voice within your soul for inner guidance. You can become distracted and delayed when you invite too many folks into your plans and your personal transformation. Their well meaning thoughts about your journey may not be what are needed for your personal transformation. You are the only one who can clearly define your true personal transformation journey. What you need may not be the same for another person.

Watch judgments of yourself and others. Many told me that I was losing too much weight or that I needed to do something else, but it was not right for me. As I was preparing for my fiftieth birthday, I saw on national TV that a model search had been held in New York City for women over 40. I thought I could have done it, but I missed it. Wanting to find out more, I went to the store and bought a copy of *More* magazine to get the telephone number. I called to find out when the next one would be held. The lady on the other end told me in one year. At that time I remembered the personal goals I had set for myself when I was young. At 12 years of age I was looking in magazines saying, "I should be in here. I want this career." Here I was a black teen who didn't understand what a model did, but wanted it for myself. It was my dream or my destiny from birth, I think. I didn't like academics in school, but I loved all the performing arts and creative writing classes I took. When I was a child, my learning style had not yet been identified, so I was bored. My mother was a teacher who didn't understand the creative world that I surrounded myself with. I studied all the magazines I got my hands on. At 14 years old I went into a department store to find a national teen model search for my age in *Seventeen* magazine. I came home and told my mother I wanted to enter this contest.

A neighbor who lived across the street happened to be a professional photographer. Since the entry called for a full-body and a swimsuit shot, I had him take the first shots, but not the swimsuit because of my fear. I got a letter back from the magazine and found that I was a finalist; however, they still wanted a swimsuit shot. My fear was that I looked like a Black Twiggy with no curves. I didn't have any guidance from a parent, nor from the photographer. I had no one to say, "You look wonderful as you are." I messed up the shot by putting on a wig, but sent it along with a signed release form from my mother. They liked my soft, childlike look; however, that was the end of that journey.

On the other hand, as an adult looking back the timing was not perfect. Many things could have gone wrong: sex, drugs, money, etc. when I was a teenager who wanted to model. So as an adult I have forgiven my

mother and myself for failures of the past. I perceived my dreams of
modeling as lost. When growing up I receive no guidance and direction to perfect my artistic talents. After high school I went to fashion merchandising school and started to work. My personal goals were to work in window dressing and finally open up a store of my own. I met my now ex-husband, and the dreams I had slowly began to fade away. In time I got a job in retail, but he said I loved it more than I loved him. By the time I started to have children I had lost my dream. I had forgotten it, though I had no regrets. There were no memories of my dreams; I must have repressed them while married. I never thought I would be given a second chance to give birth to my ideas, dreams, and purpose again. When I was young, I thought a modeling career stopped at a young age. Could this passion for fitness at 50 have been my dream from God all along, I asked myself. When I was getting fit to turn 50, the long buried dream resurfaced even stronger. Being the co-creator of my destiny with my sacred source, the dream became alive
again even stronger.

I had started designing clothes. Finally, with the new goals in my heart, mind, and soul,

everything began to become clearer. I realized that now I could enter a national contest for my mature age group. My fitness challenges started to take on another level. I wanted to measure
right up with others. While my dreams were re-emerging I thought, "Why wait for the national contest?" People were telling me I looked like a model, so I hit the streets of Nashville. Who would have thought years ago that at 50, I would be preparing for a performing arts career? Once I started seeking a place where I could get work, a new path or commitment for opportunities opened up. Was this the plan of God all along? Because of my faithfulness to get moving, like Carnegie's explanation on fear, my dreams became reality.

I love going to the gym even more now that I am on a personal mission to get fit for performing. I am now a size 8/10, BMI 26, and my weight, a year later, is 165 pounds. As I look back, it was an interesting experience to look for modeling agencies in Nashville to take me on as a model. Because I was on fire to perform I thought everything would be so easy. I was so wrong! There are positives and negatives in everything that we attempt. The key is to go through the trials or obstacles put in front of you and not get caught in the middle.

Looking through the telephone book for agencies I found several, but I needed pictures. One day while sitting at a stoplight I ran into the old photographer I had when I was a teenager. When we pulled over, I told him about my goals and the national contest. He explained that he and his wife were about to start working at a well known agency very soon. The next week he took some photos. I was excited and ready. This photographer also thought I aged myself to look older, but I didn't agree and left him alone.

An appointment was made at another well known agency, where I took my pictures and told my age, 50. My first disappointment came when the manager said that I was too old; they used younger women for music videos.

My self-esteem was low when I left. Now what? My old photographer wanted me to come to the office where he and his wife were working. I just didn't have the money to pay the tuition. Later on he called to offer me dance lesson opportunities for a fee, but I was attending the YMCA, which offered free dance lessons to members. He said if I took these lessons I could audition for music videos. I almost signed up, but changed my mind. I became confused and unsure about what to do, so I did nothing. I made a few more calls to schools and agencies in faith. One out of five returned my call. I went out for another audition and was the only one there over 30!

I finally decided on a school and enrolled. As soon as clients heard that I was in school, they started giving me clothes that they thought I would need for basic modeling. I was also designing or remaking clothes. Most of the clothes were classics, and there were lots of them.

I finally got a call back to attend, and my tuition was financed. The talent scout and I met. She was warm, friendly, and helpful. I asked, "What about my age?" She wanted to know my background, so I told her that I had a skin care and massage license. I also told her about my
unfulfilled dreams of childhood modeling. She said she knew something about me was different. She also said that I probably would get bored because there was a lot of skin care and makeup instruction, since I was a skin care professional already. Her

suggestion was that I should assist the teacher at some point. The booking agent found out about me and sent me on an audition the first week. It was for a music video, and I got the part at the age of 50. I really was focused at the gym to get weight off and to tone up. I started giving my old clothes away because they were too big.

There was a local over-40 model search she thought I should enter in our city. She went on to say that as they went through their files there were no other women strong enough to enter. I said I would. First prize was a two-year contract with an established talent agency in Nashville. I sent in photos and the requested information, which included a small statement on why I wanted to win the contest. This is what I wrote: *For over 39 years I have known I was meant to model, even after six children. Now that I am mature I have the confidence I lacked in my youth.*

I also sent in a headshot and a full-body shot. It was now time to attend my first class. Orientation books, tote bags, and makeup brushes were given out. I was in a room of kids, teens, and young adults. I felt out of place because even though I looked

younger, I was old enough to be their
mother. At the end of the night we walked
on the runway and were also told not to
wear
jeans and tennis shoes. The next time I went
to TV print. I didn't care about the TV print
class. The teacher was okay, but I was
unsure of TV. I wanted to learn runway first,
but I told no one. The next time I had
another runway teacher. This time the
feeling was totally different. I had an uneasy
feeling. She found out I worked out at the
gym. She put her hands on my body to
correct my posture. Then the younger
women spoke up to me while I was on the
runway telling me how to walk. I thought
her class was so out of order that my head
started to hurt. When it was over, I thought I
should give up the nicer, kinder, and
talented other runway teacher, who taught
on Saturdays not on Tuesdays.

After class I just sat in my car, frustrated. I
wanted to quit. After a while I left and went
to get something to eat. While sitting in the
restaurant, a man came over. I didn't know
him, and if he was an angel or not, he saved
my career. He asked, "Who did you used to
model for?" I asked him to say it again. I
thought then, I am going back and recreating
my dream. I went to the talent scout, who

brought me in and complained about the teachers and my experience. They took me out of TV print for a while and moved me to the more talented teacher. Then the director of the school quit, and I could feel the tension in the building. Everything changed immediately. I was really ready to quit and go somewhere else, but I gave the school another chance. They brought in an interim director, but the tension was still there.

I thank God for my time in the gym working out the frustrations because even though I had a desire to perform and was willing to learn, tests of faith, obstacles, and disappointment presented themselves to me daily. I had a choice to throw in the towel or to persevere with the help of God and a few friends. Many times I left that building frustrated and in dismay about how things were
being handled in class, but I just had to remember why I was there. My personal purpose and dream sustained me. I could easily have given in to what I thought was really happening to me and around me, but I had to set my sights higher and remember the end results. At the same
time I was having trouble, I was learning the skill for the runway.

I didn't understand the talented teacher's instructions for the catwalk. I was talking to a friend about it, and she suggested that it may have to do with some negative experiences from my childhood that I needed to let go of. I wrote a letter to a family member about the experiences, hurts suffered and let everything go. I finally got the walk and felt free from the leftover baggage that I had been carrying all those years. I did it! These were some of the emotional toxins I had held onto for a long time.

I said good-bye to the past to say hello to my future with a peaceful state of mind. With this new way of thinking, things began to change.

Clothes began pouring in: coats, shoes, jewelry, and wigs—you name it! My clients gave me luggage, dresses with price tags, shirts, and three pairs of brand new high heeled shoes. I wanted my style to be vintage, and clothes came out of nowhere—some from people, some from yard sales. I was also given an old computer to write this book with. I added everything up and it totaled $28,000.

A client keeps telling me about the "Law of Attraction and the movie the Secret," and I would say, "What's that?" I received a call that I was one of the six finalists in the local contest. I was beside myself. I lived with a sense of gratitude for all things that seem bad or good and gave thanks always. I just knew this was going to be easy, but when we went on the midday TV show, the drama began. What I have been sharing are insights filtered by my perspective and views of my situation. I have tried to write objectively about my training at school and about the local contest. Everything that appears negative, to be a hardship, or presents deep trials often has a bigger picture at the end if you stay on the course. Many times there are numerous blessings received and achievements to be accomplished. Everyone's coping skills are different, but once you apply resilience to a stressful situation and use a realistic perspective, you come out on top.

At this time I was still trying to get paid by the school for a music video I had shot 4 months earlier. I stopped paying tuition, which I felt was in all fairness, whether wrong or right. I had been asking and calling the corporate office for six weeks. I was getting disappointed in the school's actions in every way. My frustrations showed up in many ways, mainly headaches and muscle pain. I had to go to the doctor and receive massages because of the stress-induced headaches. The gym outlet was working, but there was still a high amount of stress. I had to learn to manage my strong emotions and feelings without suppressing them.

Once we six received our finalist calls we appeared on the local TV station. My thoughts were that this is a lifelong dream of accomplishment for me. The owner of the talent agency, who was offering one of us a two-year modeling contract, was there. Before one of us would be awarded the two-year contract, we all had to be in a fashion show. That was when he would name the winner.

His agency was also going to take photos of the winner, place them on the agency's web site, and send her off to the national over-40 contest being held in New York. He held interviews with each of us. It amazed me that even without knowing us, he would tell us about his negative behaviors. He shared how no one wanted to go out for auditions when he called. When it was my turn, I thought we were having a wonderful conversation. During the interview he learned that I was attending a modeling school. He told me he didn't want his talent working for anyone but him.

Finally we had our first practice. Before the practice I hired my talented runway teacher, who had already quit the school, to tutor me. At the first practice some of the talent agency's clients were there. The owner fussed and blew off steam for an hour and a half. He did not care that we were there listening to the dirty laundry of his business. He made one comment that if they didn't go out and get auditions, he could not eat. That stuck in the back of my mind. But when one of his clients asked him a simple question, he raised his voice and said he didn't hear them. He went on to say, "Can't you all phrase a question, and talk so I can hear? You all are actors. Is this what you do in an audition? Is this why you can't get booked?" I was shocked how forward and harshly he spoke to the clients, who were making money for him.

We were told that we had to sell $200 worth of ads for the fashion show in three weeks. We had to sell that amount or else. Under pressure I paid most of my own and asked family members to donate to the event. I did what I had to do, but it was very stressful and financially straining, since I didn't know beforehand what this contest was going to cost. But I wanted to complete the experience to see if I truly wanted a performing arts career. This was my heart's desire, so I started doing yoga every morning to ground, center, balance, and relax my soul's emotions and fears.

I received a phone call from a dear friend warning me about his agency and not to sign with him. I said that my goals were higher than that local contest and his agency. Another one called to say that her daughter was once involved with that same talent agency and that she didn't recommend it.

One day while sitting at practice, God's spirit spoke to me. I was told to give away all my clothes that I had not worn for two years and all my low-heel shoes. I thought I was crazy. Also the Spirit told me that this was not the place where I would stay, but that I was gaining experience from it all. My closets were empty, even though caring people had given me clothes. Once I figured out my style—vintage and classic—I started receiving that type of clothing. I gave the old clothing away as I was told, not knowing how I was going to replenish my wardrobe.

My runway teacher was pregnant and benefited from most of them. She told me I needed a black dress. I told her I didn't have the money for it. I took a load of clothing to another woman over 50 starting a new career in performing arts. She was thrilled out of her mind. She asked me to wait a minute, that there was a dress in her car that would fit me. It was a black dress with a BeBe's label and a price tag of $265. It was beautiful and I could wear it. I took it to the dry cleaner's and when I went back to get it, it was gone. The establishment said they could not find
it. I called, but they would not return my calls. I called the police to file a report, and the manager of the dry cleaner's called me back. She asked me to give her two weeks. One day while driving in the area and I hadn't heard from them, a thought crossed my mind that I should by go there. When I did, she said she found the dress on the floor. I got my dress back. I was very thankful because I didn't have that much money to buy another one. It was also a gift of confirmation. The manifestation of that black dress told me that the dress was for me. The "Law of Attraction" was at work

again. Harm was probably intended but positive came out of the so-called problem.

It was time for another practice. I was still working and attending modeling school and cleaning out the things in my closets. I felt as though I was giving birth, but this time it was to my unfilled desires and dream. While in practice the owner started to talk again for an hour. Before he started, he told his clients to take notes. I put my hand to my face, thinking. He stopped and asked if I had a question. I said no. Later I did it again. This time I needed to use the restroom, but I really didn't want to leave. He asked again, and I told what I needed. Of course he made a smart remark.

We all were chatting about nothing when he raised his voice and screamed, "Be quiet! Stop talking!" You could never appear friendly or even talk when he was around. He wanted total control. He still hadn't told us how much the tickets were and what he required of us, even when we asked. Repeatedly he went over the time for us to arrive for fitting and such. Someone asked a question, and I answered the question quickly without thinking. He told me I was out of order and that he was tired of me doing that. I said to him again that I was sorry, that I was wrong.

Eventually we were ready to walk on the runway, and now it was my time. I was not going to let his actions fill me with fear and intimidation; that was what he loved. I hit the runway with confidence and knowledge, and when I got to the bottom where he was, he clapped. He really helped me let go of my fears of what people thought about me in this business. I gave him an I-am-in-control-of-me-not-you look. I returned back up and did the same.

He got on a young college student because of her shoes. He belittled her in front of everyone. She put her head down. I asked her if she knew how to take off a jacket on the runway. She said, "What do I know? I just get yelled at." I thought, how sad. She also shared with another person that she didn't have money for shoes. That person offered to bring her some shoes at next practice. I knew that he and his agency were not the right place for my soul. If I hadn't been in the contest and able to witness his interactions, I would have signed with him before researching his agency.

Sometimes you need to do research, pray, and test an agency before getting involved. By now another group of performers, some of whom I had known for years, were telling me not to get involved with his agency. I asked why I shouldn't. They told me he didn't treat his clients with respect or fairness. I took their warnings to heart. I felt God was directing them to tell me the truth before I made a mistake. I asked them what was I to do if I won. It was then that I started to pray not to win.

During practice he asked a question: What do you not want to see when you take off a jacket? One client answered the seams; I said the lining. In front of everyone he said, "Modeling School 101," instead of, "That's correct, Carol." Then he was looking at our shoes. I knew that my teacher had prepared me correctly. He said that no one was wearing the correct shoes. I stood in silence and didn't get caught up in his crazy drama. About 30 minutes later he came back and said that another woman and I did. I knew this already, so I didn't sweat it. You learn to pick and choose your battles. I thought, this is not worth it, but I knew God had designed me to be a finalist. I couldn't understand what the heck was occurring. I was so nervous I ran my cell phone bill up. Thank God for the gym, which was my outlet to help me solve my problems and release my tension. I also used my spiritual practices, which included meditation and prayer.

When I told my well meaning friends and family members I could not win, they thought I was just being negative about the situation. I learned to stop talking about it. But I prayed not be a winner. I had a dream that one of the women was going to win. It was now time to sell tickets, which were $20. They couldn't be returned. Our children and spouses had to buy a ticket as well.

Now fears of *what if* had crept up into my spirit. I couldn't sleep; something didn't feel right. My faith was a minute-by-minute thing at this time. A dear friend was afraid for me not taking the prize if I won. I knew I couldn't. People in the industry don't speak very openly about others in the same profession.

He sent the six finalists to a music video shoot. I thought we were getting paid. We when we got there, they told us to put a zero (0) on the line for the amount. No one had told me. I had left my massage practice for this shoot. We did the music video, but none of us was happy about not getting paid.

He wasn't there, but one of the finalists shared with me how she felt about the program. She said she didn't know if she wanted it. I told her she was going to win. She said, "I thought you." I told her no, that I had too many options and he didn't like that. She said she told her husband after the way he had talked to me, she didn't know if she would accept the offer. I told her she needed to explore her options and understand how other agencies work. I also shared with her things that I was told.

I was nearly finished with the modeling school. The runway teacher, the booking agent, a secretary, another director, and another teacher had quit. This was now five months later. (I still have not received my payment for the music video.) Another group of staff members arrived.

The experience was positive; the school's atmosphere felt different again. The school's new director held in-house auditions for students to work out in the community for the school. Auditions were held, and I made the cut. I was in the runway class afterwards. The teacher met with us one on one, and when he asked what my ambitions were, I said I wanted to be a mature model and had entered the national contest to become one of the winners in New York. He asked to see my photos and said he saw my next set of photos to enter in classic clothing. I asked, "How do you know what's in my closet?" That was what was left. I was grateful and thankful for his youthful insight. He was only twenty-six years old. I shared with him how this was my childhood dream and about my fashion merchandising degree; that this was all I ever wanted to do with my life—to be in performing arts. It had been on hold for over 35 years and now my soul was ready. My children are grown and no longer did I have anyone else to hold me back.

After this contest was over my thoughts were about my next step on my dream path. Could I work if I didn't win the local? How badly I wanted this type of performing art, I thought. My career as a skin care professional and massage therapist was so rewarding—why add anything else? I searched deep within my soul. This had been buried within me for over 39 years. Regardless of the storms I had to endure, I was willing to sail into my destiny. The doors were opened up to me, and I knew there were other paths for me to walk.

I spoke with the runway teacher, and she told me about another agency. I called and made an appointment. I also made an appointment for my new photos to be taken to enter the national contest and for my portfolio. I did this all before the contest was over. I had had a dream of the winner, so I was free. I thanked God because I felt as if a weight had been lifted.

Remembering what God had told me about my destiny, the dream of the winner, and remembering what the winner (in my dream) had told her husband, my confidence improved. Inner peace took over my fears.

Th e modeling school I was attending still owed me for the video shoot done five months prior. Then the new director called and asked me to work in the field for the school for less than minimum wage. Although I wasn't happy, I said okay. I thought, they already owed me; but I said okay anyway. I must have been in good standing with the school to get this job.

As I said before I didn't pay my tuition for two months in what I thought was fairness. I kept calling, but no one in the main headquarters returned the call. One day, however, I received a call from the school loan office asking about my payment. I told them when the modeling school/talent office paid me, they would get their money. The chief loan officer told me he had nothing to do with that problem, and neither did he offer a solution to help me receive the overdue payment. I said okay and hung up. He called back and said that I hung up on him and that he was calling the headquarters of the agency/school to have my records pulled. He stated that I would no longer be able to do a job for the school and demanded that I repay the loan in full within 10 days.

Next the new director called to tell me I was no longer welcome on the school campus and that I could not work for them again. She claimed she didn't know why. The next day I called the home office to tell them what happened and to ask for an e-mail address to inform them. I got no response. I called to get the name of the chief loan officer. He asked what I thought I would gain by complaining to the president of the agency's company and others. I told him, "I asked you for your name, nothing more." He said I would never get back in school, even though I didn't complete the program, and I told him I didn't need the school or the agency. Within the next week I received the overdue check.

All the while this outside negativity was occurring the local contest was still going on. As I was driving, I clearly heard God speak to me and say, "They are distractions to you right now—these negative influences." We were told to be at the fashion show five hours ahead of time for fitting, hair, makeup, and the test show. A party was being held three hours before the show began. The talent agent showed up an hour and a half later. Nothing was done until he got there. He was not in a good mood. There was cursing and screaming and no professionalism in front of all of us, including children and their parents. No one said a word; we just walked around on eggshells.

One friend shared that maybe this was in preparation for other fashion levels to come. I wasn't sure what was actually happening, but I still wanted a career in fashion. I wanted to teach, model, and design clothes. I didn't want to be surrounded by the negative atmosphere. I needed to build up more fortitude, resilience, and determination along with a deep sense of my sacred source. This was a major test of faith in my childhood passion. It was what I wanted to manifest in my future. After gaining enough experience I wanted to create a program for women over 40 who wanted to get back into the performing arts. Many women had started asking how I got back in shape. In just seven months they were asking, and all of them were over 40.

At the fashion show the winner was the one in my dream. I even did her makeup because the makeup artist was late. I thought that where much has been given, much is required.

At my new photographer's studio I shared with him I wanted to work with women over 40. He asked if I meant lifestyle models/actresses. I said, "Yes!" It was now time to go to a new talent agent. She took me because she liked my photos. She asked me about losing weight, and I told her about my goals to work with women over 40. My photos were added to her web site. While no money was paid out, she told me up front how much percentage would be taken for a job.

Within three months of signing I have been on three auditions, two music videos, one fashion show, and a national commercial. For the first video she paid me within three weeks of shooting. I called and thank her. I have heard horror stories about different agencies from several sources. All I can say is don't sign a contract without researching the agency and other options. Every agency that sounds good may not be the place for you. Do your research. Pay out nothing without first checking them out.

One day my new agent called me for an audition. When I went out, my car had been repossessed. The car was gone! No one had called to warn me. You would think that I hadn't paid every time. I admit that I had missed two payments; however, not in a row. They said they would release the car to me with half the money owed. I had already bought two other cars with them. I assumed that I had a relationship with them.

With my mind made up, I called someone to come and take me to the place where the auditions were being held. All the way there she preached to me about my finances. After a while I asked her to be quiet so I could center myself and walk into the place. I walked in and did my audition. While riding the bus home, I thought, Determination! What makes up your character? Do you know where your help comes from? Your sacred source. I said to myself, "My Higher Power is my source of strength and my mind is firmly made up. I want to work in the performing arts." Before now I was always backstage or in the artist's home doing a massage. I never thought about being center stage. When I finished massage school eight years before, I knew I was to be doing massages in the entertainment field, and I have. The tables have turned or perhaps this was the divine plan all along?

Two days later I got a call from the agents to do a film. She never knew what happened to my car. Many friends, my sister, and my children were supportive during my misfortune, or so we thought.

One Sunday I woke up and said, "God, I answer the calling to write this book and work with others who want to get into the performing arts, to help them understand the world, prepare them for the task with opened eyes." I went to church that morning; the sermon was "Called into Greatness." I said, "God, I get the message." At that time I started writing. I felt impressed to call the gospel radio station to share my determination to be in the performing arts even if I had no car, which makes it hard to get around in Nashville. I surrendered to my situation and put my trust in God. I have no regrets, no complaints. I am grateful for everything and the experience I've gained. The radio disc jockey asked, "Baby, do you need a car?" I said, "I don't know because I have resolved to walk or to use public transportation." She gave me a number to call. She also said that what appeared to hurt me God was going to use for my good. Within two days the car salesman called; my loan was approved at the dealership. I walked around the lot and thought, that's a cute PT Cruiser, but I can't get that one. I limited God and myself right away. As I sat in his office he said God has something for you to do. He said he only worked the prestigious car lot on referrals, not off the lot. He told me God was the only one who knew my heart. He said the people he gets have been struggling for a long time, but that things were about to change for them. I told him of my desire to teach and work as a mature lifestyle model. He was shocked. We walked the lot, and he showed me seven cars, but said that he knew which one I was getting. He said it looked like me. He showed me the one God had picked out for me, a 2005 PT Cruiser. I was in shock and felt bad about putting limitations on my scared source and myself. The car was one year old and had 26,900 miles. My clients, friends and family were shocked at the favor I gained over the situation.

A few weeks later, on October 20, I dreamed I was teaching runway. Three weeks later a woman who was in the contest called me and asked where I was working. I was surprised to hear from her because we had had only one conversation in those two months. She informed me that she had just opened a model/talent agency and asked if I would come teach there. I told her I'd be there in two hours. My first class was three days later.

Where much is given, much is required to be given back to help others on their path. Resilience is about springing back after you've faced troubles, stress, and setbacks. In order to persevere and to follow your path's purpose you must remove limitations and remember your sacred source and the role models gone before you. Dr. Martin Luther King, Jr.'s dream wasn't fulfilled until after his death. The change started; seeds were planted. He knew that hatred would be removed soon.

A close friend shared the Scripture in Genesis about Joseph, the dreamer, who had many dreams. He shared with his family and others that he would become a great person and have favor with God as a ruler. His brothers didn't like the fact that he would receive greatness and sold him as a slave. They didn't want to bow down to their brother. They envied him; they did not want him to have greatness. The brothers wanted revenge, acted with evil intentions, and wanted to hurt Joseph. They didn't destroy his faith, his dreams, and his favor with God. Later his brothers had to receive much needed grains and food from him. He forgave them. The dreamer held onto his dream and lived it out with acceptance from God.

How many times have we had unfulfilled dreams?

Have you had a dream/purpose and shared it too quickly with a person, and then they shot it down? Or did the person try to beat you to the dream you envisioned, but it didn't work for them? Do you have the self-discipline to endure to the end? How's your optimism? Does another
person's unwanted or incorrect advice leave you confused? What I have learned is to dig

deep inside my soul to see what it is that is truly my soul's purpose. Most of the time, you can only design the purpose or dream. The dream has been laying fertile, waiting to bloom in time and in the perfect season for you. Are we too old to implement the dreams/visions that are within our hearts and souls? Is it your season yet? I say no. You are never too old to develop and dream. I am over 50 and finally living my dreams. It's my season and soul's purpose. Can you say that? If your answer is no, plan today to recharge your soul's purpose for your own happiness. It may be your season, too.

Everything worth anything is not gained easily, but it is manageable to achieve along with the help of your sacred source. When the negative actions appear on the scene to distract you from reaching your goals, keep your eyes on the realm of possibility and your sacred source. Remove all limits you place on yourself, on others, and on God because God works through people. At this writing, I am teaching at my friend's agency three weeks after my dream.

My daughter said about my new car that God showed me favor. Favor is defined this way: a kindness done by others through God; an approval; a condition of being

highly approved; and a gift to show
fondness or more than fair treatment. Rev.
Michael Beckwith, the Spiritual Director
of Agape International Spiritual Center in
California, preached a sermon on Impossible
Dream (or Why Have One at All?): the First
and Last of It. Basically, dream big or don't
have the dream at all; just forget it.

Our Spiritual Leader at Unity for Positive
Living in Old Hickory, Tennessee,
introduced the words of the song at the
beginning of this chapter. I could not stop
crying once I heard this song. The part about
everything I've ever seen, lost, or won now
is what got me sobbing. God has
allowed me to go through the valley
experiences and witness with my eyes, only
to find there were better days already
fulfilled if I just were still and waited. Next I
thought I lost my black BeBe dress, my car,
my education, and family only to realize that
it wasn't a reality. I am a blessed woman
worthy of all good things under the heavens.
Look at the manifestation of my new car, the
clothes, and my will, winning as a finalist.
Some would say, "Carol, you're just
lucky." I say "No, very blessed and working
along with my source. I am a winner
regardless of any outcomes!"

Chapter 4
In Due Season

To everything there is a season, a time for
every purpose
under the heaven:
A time to be born and a time to die;
A time to plant and a time to pluck up what
has been
planted;
A time to kill and a time to heal;
A time to break down and a time to build up;
A time to weep and a time to laugh;
A time to mourn and a time to dance;
A time to cast away stones and a time to
gather stones
together;
A time to embrace and a time to refrain from
embracing;
A time to get and a time to lose;
A time to keep and a time to cast away;
A time to rend and a time to sew;
A time to keep silence and a time to speak;
A time to love and a time to hate;
A time for war and a time for peace.
Ecclesiastes 3:1-8

One definition of the word *season* is a
suitable or fit time. When we are preparing
to fulfill our purpose, there are suitable, fit
times for each of us. Have you felt it's your

suitable time to co-create your purpose under the heaven?

One must be willing and open-hearted to answer the Spirit's whisper within the soul to say yes. It's all in due time or your season; changes occur on this path many times. Seasons can be short, long-term, or with us for a lifetime.

Below are some insights into the word *season* that I hope you will take into your heart and spirit for a better understanding of your mission and passion.

• In *season* - at the right or proper time. May I ask if it is your right time to prepare or to commit to your soul's purpose? Have you defined your soul's purpose?

• Out of *season* - give interest or character to; make fit for use by a period of keeping or treatment. Many times you must wait out of season so to say, while God is allowing your character to build. This will make you fit for your season and grant you knowledge and insight into your missions.

• *Seasoning* - something that gives a better flavor or character. Have you noticed that smoked meat tastes better than regular meats? The flavor is the result of an aging process. If you have been waiting like me to live out your purpose for many years, your flavor is probably more developed in order to give to others and yourself.

• Last *season's* ticket: a ticket or pass entitling the holder to certain privileges for the season or a
period specified. Your sacred source has a pass entitling you to your privileges, to achieve your
life's journey. Open your heart to receive the gift of service to mankind. It's your gift from source to have the right to be happy and to have the joy that comes with serving.

Do you have a certain privilege to develop your personal soul's journey? It's now my season for a performing arts career, which has been in the birthing stage within my soul for 39 years. The dreams were buried inside my soul, forgotten, but I now remember my true purpose and
destiny. I am the ticket holder; this is my period specified by my sacred source and myself.

Because I had a buried desire to perform in my soul, it was laid to rest. All the while my interest along with my character has developed to carry out the desired results. I'm now seasoned, free and willing to give in the service I so desired as a youth. My memory has awakened to the dreams. As a seasoned adult woman, I am fulfilling my soul's purpose with better clarity than in my youth. I lacked guidance, support, maturity, growth, and confidence when

I was young and wanted this career. I was introduced to the arts early on and still have a burning desire to live it out, even though it has not all been a rose garden. I have learned and grown, and ultimately that's all that really matters. We all have our proper time and we all have different purposes.

What matters is that we work toward accomplishing our destiny, no matter how long the mission takes. It is ours to do. One may come from the North, another from the West; you may be in the East, I am in the South. What matters is that we are walking the path designed by God and by ourselves. This will entitle us to certain privileges with God as co-designer of our soul's purpose.

Have you sought your sacred source to help you understand your soul's path? In the morning when you awake, ask for Spirit's help to go within your soul and discover your hidden talents. Ponder on the question daily for the answers. The next morning sit still for twenty minutes at least. Around 4 a.m. in the stillness, listen for answers. Listening is very important. Many times we just want to ask, ask, and ask. Get your journal and write what comes to your mind first and go from there into action.

Do you compare yourself to others instead of looking within? We look on the outside of another, but we truly don't know what they went through to get to where they are now. An African Proverb goes like this: "Building our neighbor's house will not improve the structure of our dwelling." My friend, you can't improve your holy temple (body) if you are correcting that of your friend's. Many of us do clearly understand our true purpose and mission but seek answers from others on the outside. This has been said before, "Go within." The answers you seek are not on the outside of you; they are simply within your soul.

So often I didn't have the confidence to trust my inner judgments I trusted others. I came to recognize the truth for me is within me. If only I ask, sit in the silence to hear the still small voice inside, then action is needed. Do you have the patience, spiritual insight, reliance, fortitude, and determination for your path? How bad do you want to accomplish your lifelong dreams and goals, whatever they might be? Are you willing to give up something in your life to gain a sense of who you are, to grow and develop into a better person on the earth and give back what you have learned to others? Learn to laugh at your mishaps and so-called problems; this was a hard task for me. Now I have developed the gift of laughter and learned to identify a distraction and dismiss it, like the call from the chief loan officer at the school or my car being repossessed. Move on, learn the lessons, and grow into a *seasoned* person with focus on your soul's journey.

Your steps have been ordered and you must follow the path where they may lead. Destiny's calling your soul now. There was a popular song recorded by Quincy Jones, "Everything Must Change, and Nothing Stays the Same." The earth and the planets are in constant change. We must change as well because nothing in our life or on earth stays the same. Grow! Changes in season are very different in different parts of the world. In Africa there are wet and dry periods. Such has been my life. Once my marriage ended, I was dry and in need of tender loving care. At the time I didn't know I had to nurture myself; no one else could do that job for me but me. The same is true for every human being on this planet. I felt brittle and had a hardness of my soul and spirit because my soul was dry. I had just received my massage license without knowing if I could make a good living for my children and myself. I had not worked before to pay any bills, but I was willing to try, even though for me the fear was real. I had to refocus my mind off of the fear and doubt into what I wanted to create. Everything I thought was real wasn't real at all. I realized that I wanted to work, I needed to work. I was getting calls to do massages for entertainers in their homes, backstage, in their offices, and at recording studios. I thought that this was my lot in life. I never thought I would be center stage again. This was the limitation I had placed on myself. We are spiritual beings living in a human experience; we are unlimited.

Then a wet period followed with blood, sweat, and tears came along as I tried to carry out my mission, but I made it work. The plan of action for nurturing myself paid off , and work started to come my way from entertainers. During this time I explored changes and their cycles, much like the seasonal changes of the earth. My leaves didn't turn yellow or fall off, but the vision to follow my path got dim at times. I had to regroup, take other risks, and keep on going.

Eventually I met the right people through prayer and seeking (action), which led to open doors. This opening happened with desires to create a service, answering the call within my soul, stepping up to the plate to assist others who needed my help, and believing that this was the right time for me—my season. Most regions in America have 4 seasons. In the Tennessee springtime we prepare the ground for planting after a cold, wet, snowy winter. Winter seasons in the northern and eastern part of the United States can be slow, cold, dark, and gloomy, a time for reflecting and resting the mind. To me this is the time for making plans, creating, and exploring new ways of doing things to get ready for planting season. Many people plant gardens of various types: herb, vegetable, fruit, or flower. They would not plant seeds unless the ground was correctly prepared by nurture and nourishment. It simply would not work; it would result in wasted energy.

Over the years while raising my children, I studied and used herbs for nourishment and healing in our home. Years later I started preparing myself for an herbal school I wanted to attend. I had already been studying herbs for over twenty-nine years. I learned to make herbal skin care products, which I used and sold. This was a nurturing need to understand the effects of herbs on the body, inside or out. Just like the ground requires nutrients, seeds, nurture, water, and patience for growing and yielding, I needed the same. I started to awaken my mind to the plan before the earth was formed, my destiny.

Some trees in Africa survive in the dryness because they have very long roots that tap into the groundwater from beneath. I became dry again after my two schoolings. After a time of wondering what's next, I sought another avenue for making money and gaining knowledge. I went to skin care school and got a degree in makeup and skin care. I thought then that this had to be all of my growth. Knowing that I was a lifelong learner as well as being self taught, this was just the beginning. My massage career was going strong and I was selling skin care products, but I felt something was still missing in my life. My children were

leaving the nest one by one. My dating life was a void. I couldn't keep a boyfriend or get a second date with anyone! People were telling me that I should have someone. I thought there was something wrong with me, but there
wasn't. I didn't know at the time that God was about to open up so many doors for me to walk through that I needed to be free and not be in a relationship until the appointed time. After being married for 21 years, I didn't know what I wanted from a special relationship. Since then I have pondered and made a clear list of qualities of what I want in a mate or in a relationship. It's very important to me to have a special man in my life, one who understands and supports my goals and achievements in my life. I don't want to lose sight of my dreams. How often do you get a
third chance? With the Spirit's help, I now believe I can have it all: career, family, and the support of a loving man in my life. Remembering that my roots are buried deep in the Holy Spirit is what kept me going along the path. This was how I received the water when I was thirsty. When I sought inner guidance for answers, through my spiritual practices such as: prayer, meditation, and good books my answers came to me. Answers also came from

insightful people who held me in great esteem.

Then my focus began to shift. I began trying to lose weight, but try as I might, I couldn't lose my belly. I got smaller, but the stress with the teenage children and money was overtaking me. As I kept praying for a less stressful atmosphere in my home, it happened. My youngest boy, a teenager, was causing a lot of stress. When I had him removed from the home, it lifted. It was challenge at my core, but it was good experience for all of us. He went to live with his dad and now I could get back on my journey to wholeness and health. You can't be healthy while living daily in stress. I felt the peace that I had done the right thing for all concerned. It was time to do more groundbreaking into my career, like preparing dirt for building a place. I now had freedom from a stressful marriage, children, and lifestyle. Things were reprogrammed into newness once I let go of things that were out of my control and opened up to the Spirit's process for me.

There was newness all around; flowers popped up from the earth. I, too, was ready to pop and develop myself. I entered modeling school after a long winter of resting and preparing for my next step. I talked with a friend and shared with her things I needed for this new path. There were certain things needed for this career that I didn't have. With the knowledge that audition clothing is usually black, she started helping me. Next another friend, without being asked, helped by giving me 11 bags of classic clothing—all in my new size 6. Remember, this process is called "The Law of Attraction," which is manifested in action. There are many books on the subject, for example, *Ask, and it is Given* by Ester Hicks and Manifesting your Destiny by Wayne Dyer.

Once I entered the modeling school, I realized that there were many lessons to learn and much leftover negative thinking to release. I began journaling my adventure. My son who is in the Army shared with me that he wants to write a book. My advice to him and also to you is to keep a journal. Write your thoughts daily, and look back to see where you have been. It may lead you to your next path or purpose; it's all in your hands. Here are some of the things I learned:

1. I was my greatest supporter. If no one else understood why and what I was doing, I did.

There was no need for explanation to others. A while back I would have spent hours trying to get others on board, but it was not their mission. Others may not understand, but as long as God and you understand, that's really all that matters at the end of the day. Live in faith and in the truth that you have a soul's purpose to fulfill and that you are called. Just answer and move forward with faith; you will get all the help you need from those who support you on your journey. Just ask the Spirit for help; in asking be willing to sit still to listen for answers. You asked, now sit still and listen. Then apply the information given to you. This principle is very important to your progression in creating what you know is for you to do on this earth.

2. I am a great person, worthy of all blessings. Old programs replayed in our heads must be renewed daily. Because of things in our childhood or difficulties on our path as human beings, we don't feel as if we deserve good in our lives, but we do. Own it and acknowledge it, find the courage to "let it float way like the air," and then go forward to accomplish it. Destiny is waiting for you to wake up with a positive new mindset. Sonny Rollins said, "What

difference does it make if you live to be a hundred, but you don't do anything?"

3. I cannot participate in the performing arts and on the runway where I struggle until I let go of the past; this is what I said to my lower self. As a child I often lacked guidance, self-esteem, and confidence to complete a task. With Spirit's help I have the source of all things needed living within me. Forgiveness has been a divine order for me at this time. Some have asked me what I had to forgive and why. In order for me to move on, I had to let go of the past as I mentioned before. You have to become a big person to forgive another and yourself for mistakes and hurt you put on others and yourself. Have you put hurts on others? Others put hurts upon me; I know I have hurt others as well and I took them on myself. I thought I was a bad person in this life. I felt God was mad at me for not being a good person and for my failures. I felt this was why things hadn't worked out for me.

It was time for me to see what had occurred in my life experiences and forgive, forget, and let go.

"He who conceals his disease cannot expect to be cured."

— African proverb

4. First I had to forgive my mom for not giving me guidance and direction in my life. I now understand that she didn't know her way either. Many parents are in too much pain. All you can do when you have children is try to give them what you lack and pray that they receive the guidance in love. I also had to forgive my God for not allowing me to become who I wanted to be, my ex-husband for stopping my growth and all the negative talk he shared, and myself for past failures and lack of self-esteem. "I can't do it," I said on the runway. It was a learned negative behavior from childhood. Facing frustration and impatience with myself, I started to receive everything I needed in my life and career. This, too, passed once I let go, let God, forgave, and moved in a positive direction. This process is called "surrendering to the Universe."

5. I will master my arts. My person, CAROL, will come out. My created true personality was buried deep within my soul. It was there suppressed. A dear friend told me I had to let the essence of my beauty come forward and release all that I had endured in the past.

"The opportunity that God sends does not wake up him or her who is asleep"
—*Senegalese proverb*

6. I can do everything I need with my sacred source's help and guidance. Before a show or audition, I meditate and do yoga. Remembering the scripture affirmation for me, *"I can do all things through Christ who strengthens me."* (Philippians 4:13) This is where I asked my sacred source to allow people to see my inner and outer beauty and talent. My mission in the performing arts is to have a smile for someone who needs to be uplifted in some way—that my God source, working through me, is there to heal them.

"When spiders unite, they can tie down a lion"
— *Ethiopian proverb*

The end of spring was when I received the call about the local over-40 model search. School had already started changes for the good and bad. Another director had gone.

During preparation for the fashion show contest I kept a journal as well. I share my insights:

1. I honor neither man nor woman above my sacred source. Oftentimes those in authority want you to bow down and worship them, whether they are talent agents, agencies, photographers, or such; respect is all that's needed.

2. Don't forget where my blessings come from. My blessings are from a Power higher than me – a sacred source. I give thanks for my sacred source's guidance, direction, renewed confidence, insight, and growth to share this information with others who have a similar interest. I hope this information empowers you to take the challenge to answer your soul's calling and purpose.

3. Don't lose your center in a stressful time. Keep focused on who you are and what you want to achieve. Distractions are a given when you are trying to focus on a specific mission in life. The car and the chief loan officer, as I said before, were big stumbling blocks for me. I could have focused on the negative picture in front of me or dismissed them for a later date. It was my choice. In silence you often find your answer. It's a still, small voice of assurance that tells you that everything will be okay, take this path. So often we don't want to hear the inner voice that is calling us to learn a new skill,

to grow, to receive information, or to give to others so that you may be a blessing. Pay close attention to your inner positive voice. Don't lose who you are in the midst of what seems to be trouble on your path. What appears one way may not be the way it really is. Have faith in your sacred source and in yourself that all things will work out for your good if you stay on the right path, your soul's purpose.

4. Release fear, stress and all negative concerns in a positive way. Meditation, prayer, and physical outlets along with forgiveness help. If help is needed, you will be directed to the source or the source will come to you. Just keep breathing and smiling.

5. Don't take on another person's stuff. Own your own stuff, no one else's. Those who you may have to work with may have deep-seated issues. Recognize the difference between your issues and theirs. In silence, pray and meditate on your issues. When you are in the midst of the situation, view it from the outside looking in. Don't respond to the problem; be still. Work on releasing your stuff and not trying to fix theirs.

6. Believe in your inner guidance. Listening to the spirit within you is necessary for success on any level. Your connection with your scared source is important. Seek, ask, knock, and then be ready to receive the answers through a still, small voice.

7. Listen only to others who give you sound advice. A friend told me that sometimes those who don't win a contest go farther than those who do because they are free to do so. This was the case for me. I am free to be with another agency and to teach.

8. I am a multi-talented woman and am open to receive from and give to others. Where much is given, much is required. Know your gifts and talents. In this, know yourself within. If you have knowledge or a way to help another, then feel free to give help.

> • If you perform, you must prepare yourself spiritually, emotionally, physically, and mentally for performance. You must create an outlet where you feel comfortable to relax, release, and stretch before performing or going in for an audition. Develop a spiritual practice that just for you.

9. Don't become defeated by the petty words of others. They are only given to distract you from your mission. Insensitive comments were made to me but I didn't react. I learned from the comments and used what I could; what I didn't need for myself I now use in my teaching.

10. You must be a team player, work peacefully with others, and keep your eyes on your goals and the end results. Help your friends and support them in their efforts when you work.

11. This one is of utmost importance: You never know who is watching you; behave as a role model. Many thought I had been doing performing arts for years before now. I was being watched by others and didn't know it. I dressed as if I were on the runway long before I mastered the art. While attending any practice or class, I dressed as if I were a model performing an art. This is very important for first impressions, which make lasting ones. Dressing for Success is most important you never know who will run into that may advance your career or need you to speak to a group.

After the fashion contest, I was exhausted from the negative stress I felt. Recovering my energy, I realized I really did want to teach. The talent agent with the fashion show made a smart remark to me after I answered a question, saying, "Modeling School 101." I thought that would be a perfect subject for a class or a pamphlet for a new student.

Silently I thanked him! After seeing how people were treated and spoken to, I thought I could help. Mentally I took notes on how things could be improved for student performance and learning. What bothered me the most was how the younger teens and adults treated the older students. Then I couldn't dismiss how one teacher treated me, when she was young enough to be my daughter. Once she found out I was doing a series of exercises, she thought I should be able to walk better. She said it out loud. I thought to myself, there has to be a better way for women over 40 who want to perform, during or after marriage or maybe they are single and just want to try something new. I could either complain or create a new approach with a safe environment and a love for students of all ages. This all stemmed from the thought I had about the modeling school I had entered in the spring. Seeing the problems of a few teachers, I saw other ways to teach.

Recently my oldest son left for the Army. When he was 12, he said he was going to be in the armed services. When he entered ninth grade, we put him in ROTC. He dropped out, even though we begged him not to do so. His ROTC officers encouraged him as well. It was his choice. He dropped out and turned to the streets and drugs for about five years. After his daughter was born, he decided to kick his drug habit. It's funny how children seem to bring out the best in us. We want to be role models for our children. He got clean from drugs, and then he turned to God for recovery and joined the Army National Guard for two years. I cried for a month before and after he left. Despite knowing this was my son's purpose, it wasn't easy for me to accept because of the wars. That's my stuff! I am dealing with it. I'm letting go and learning to surrender, knowing that God is providing everything he needs. I am his mother, human; yet I understand the spiritual side having this concept: No weapon formed against him/me/you shall prosper. (Isaiah 54:17, paraphrased.) I let go of my need to control his life path (surrender) and let God provide what I couldn't (peace along with understanding, and protection for my son). He told me his soul's purpose when he was twelve years old; I must honor his decision and support his works. I trust his knowledge of his work.

When he left for the full-time Army, I cried for three days. I asked him what made him change his service from part-time to full-time in the Army. He said, "Mom, you may not understand. No other jobs are working out. I don't feel complete until I have that Army uniform on." I said, "I do understand. I was twelve when I knew that I wanted to model and be in magazines. I am now 51 and don't feel right until I am performing on stage or in front of a camera. I do understand."

In the Bible, Joseph dreamed his dreams and after many years, he lived those dreams. His life wasn't easy. He faced many challenges, but overall he came through the tough times and didn't get stuck. My question is, are we ever too old to stop dreaming of our soul's purpose?

With all the schooling since taking on the new path after marriage, I was being nudged into the performing arts. My son's life and my own life are very similar. How about your life? We both knew our destiny at the age of 12. It doesn't matter how long it takes to get to the place we need to be. What matters is that we end up there, somehow living out our soul's purpose. For one person it may take ten years; another, 50 years. All that really matters is that we do reach our soul's purpose and fulfill our destiny with a passion in our hearts.

After receiving a new car, I received about $28,000 worth of clothes and items as well. The blessings have kept coming as a testimony that I am on the right track. My garden is yielding from seeds planted 39 years ago. Once I started modeling school at 50 and said what I needed for my career, things started manifesting in my life and have helped me not spend money that I didn't have to spend. The items manifested were out of pure desire and thoughts.

I thank God for all my blessings and even for the learning experiences, which at first appeared to be negative! As I began feeling an urge to teach, I started writing this instruction manual. I thought then that it would be some time in the distant future; however, one day I picked up my phone. It was one of the women from the local over-40 contest, who said she had just opened up a new model/talent agency. She asked if I wanted to teach. After I got over the shock, I told her on October 20, two months after the ending of the contest, that I had had a dream that I was teaching runway. She said she opened up that same week. In my dream I had my hands around the student in love and care. This happened in my class. The student did not have the confidence to walk, so I walked with her. This was based on my own experience. During the contest experience I had never said anything to the owner of the model/talent agency except hello. She watched me the whole time and I didn't know it. For this reason you must believe and act as if you have already accomplished whatever you want to achieve.

The next question she asked me came as a surprise. She said that the class was for preteens! I was preparing for women over the age of 40. I felt the call to teach and I answered the call. I said yes; I would do whatever the call was. Remember in Chapter 3 that I said I woke up one morning and answered the call to serve wherever. Later I went to the Unity church and the sermon was "Called into Greatness." I said to myself, Spirit, I get the message. When I lost my car, I got a new one. Service was being impressed upon my spirit. I cried out and said, "If you don't want me to have a car, if you want me to teach or give, I will. I just want to do what is required of me at this time." Two days later I had a car and peace was mind. I knew I was on the right path.

My spiritual leader at the Unity Church for Positive Living in Old Hickory, Tennessee, Reverend Denise Yeargin often tells us, "When the student is ready to learn, the teacher shows up." When I told my close friend about the preteen students she insightfully said, "The students must be ready because the teacher is appearing – YOU."

I took the same question to God. My answer was that it starts with children first, not adults. "Carol," the Spirit said, "how was it when you were their age and wanted to perform? What type of instruction did you receive? Did you have guidance and support?" My mission to those children is to learn all I can from them; they are my teachers. However, the other task for me is to equip them with all the knowledge and preparation they need to enter the workforce in performing arts.

I got excited about my new gift. I went into thought and prayer of what to share with the students. As I was doing my kickboxing and spinning classes, the lesson to share started to unfold. Spirit led me to ask the children, how did your parents get you to school that day? Did you have any road problems? Were there any setbacks from a wreck? Did your parents get lost and have to ask for directions? Some people get frustrated when they get lost," I shared. "Did you face that issue and want to give up?" As we continued the discussion, I said what really mattered was that we all ended up there at our performing arts school together. We all came to the same place from all different directions but ended in the appointed place together at the same time.

So we all have different unique talents to share with the world. We may be on the path together or separate; it doesn't matter. What's important is that we end up in the performing arts career of a lifetime if it is truly ours to own. Each of us is different. We all have a unique calling, yet we are all of the same mind. We don't all have to go on the same path to achieve our soul's purpose.

My son could have gone to the full-time Army long before now. He chose not to until the appointed time for him. What matters is that he's on that path now. He was prepared for the Army with two years of part-time; his character was building. He never lost sight, even when he endured many years running from the call. By using drugs. If you lose sight, make a U-turn and start over again. Don't become distracted or discouraged by what seem to be setbacks, roadblocks, or detours. You have talents and gifts to share with others. When someone has been given much, much will be required in return (Luke 12:48). One day the children that God has entrusted in my care will mature and *season* to adults. Hopefully they will remember our journey together. Just like the old song recorded by Quincy Jones says, "Everything changes; nothing stays the same." Winter turns to spring. A wounded heart will heal. Never too much too soon. The young become old and the mysterious does unfold; that's the way of time. No one and nothing goes unchanged. Nothing stays the same. That's the way of time. Everything must change. My wounded heart has healed over time; how about yours? We must become as little children: willing, adaptable, open-hearted, non-judgmental, and eager to want to know and be examples to others. They embrace change, they try new ideas, and they love learning new skills. They are our teachers if would let them. Children let their lights shine!

In closing, I have shared with you about the suitable due season that was designed for me. After ending my marriage, my dry season, I thought I was only to work as a massage therapist backstage, not center stage. Little did I know that my sacred source had allowed me to go through many storms, valleys, and wet/dry/cold/hot seasons in order for me to reach my fit time, just as my son had to do. Thirty-nine years later, I am working as a performing arts teacher and mature model, creating my own clothes, and sharing all my God-given talents. We are never too
old to live out our dreams as long as the desire is there. My due season is now. I thank God for the free will, the knowledge, the timing, and the planting seasons. I am co-creating along with my sacred source here under the heavens my purpose right now.

. . . a time to plant and a time to pluck up that which is planted. **Ecclesiastes 3:2b**

Chapter 5
Destiny is Calling Your Soul
*Walk the path of your destiny with purpose
and an open
heart. – Chinese proverb*

People have asked what their destination in life or their purpose is. How do you know if you are in your right purpose or calling? Are they able to co-create their sacred destiny with the Universal God? Is it that they just answer to demands from God, giving up their free will? Is God a demanding God? I believe I co-created with God, the creator of all things and of my desired destinies. The definition of destiny is what happens in spite of all efforts to change or to prevent it. Once my car was taken back I had no transportation and I could have decided not to go to the audition, but I was determined not to miss it. I asked someone to take me all the way, and the person gave me unwanted advice. I rode the bus home. While there, the Spirit whispered to me and said it wanted to see how determined I was and what kind of stuff I was made of. I got the part in the music video. No matter what was occurring, I didn't allow the changes to prevent the mission I had set to change my destiny. During my first year of marriage, I asked my husband and myself why I am here at this time. What am I to do with my life? Of course he didn't understand. He just wanted a wife and a mother for his unborn children. I had childhood dreams that I wanted to see happen, even though I had neither guidance nor support in the path I needed to take. As he saw it I was well provided for, even though I had just received a fashion degree. After 4 years of marriage I felt the calling of our children to come to earth.

Do you believe in your soul's destiny? If you do, that's all that truly matters. It's between God, the creator, and you. While creating this book I was sent the help from earthly angels to assist me on this path of writing. If you have a calling to serve, just know that you will be given everything you need to complete the task at hand. Just let the Spirit know through prayer, meditation, thoughts, and spiritual practice. I saw what I needed, asked, pondered, and kept the thought within my soul. Go within yourself.

Do you hear, feel, or see a calling? Maybe it's time to start your family. Don't be afraid to take a risk. Seek guidance from your sacred source. Follow your heart and your soul's own way. Let go of fears that only hold your life back in a tunnel; release and apply your faith and your belief system, and you will see light at the end of the tunnel.

Forget the past; it's over. Look straight ahead. This is a brand-new day with a great future in store. Rejoice in it. Embrace it, welcoming the newness, and changing your thought patterns. Take the time to write a few goals you would like to accomplish. Destiny is calling your soul's purpose; it's your season now. Answer it today. What's burning in your heart and soul? Think, sense, feel, and acknowledge it.

Write:

Purpose is something one has in mind to get, intention. As you read this chapter you may be asking yourself, what was the purpose of my learning how to sew or learning other skills that I have, yet not using them? Have you heard the old saying, use it or lose it? That's a phrase that refers to the God-given talents and abilities that you have been entrusted with on this earth. Many times I thought I would never again use my fashion skills or model. This was my own limited thinking and the thoughts of the past that modeling stops around the age of twenty. I did want to create and develop forms, design, and art in clothing. Now because of our diets and knowledge of health, people are living better and longer, and there is a market for mature actors and models. I changed my diet and lifestyle when I was twenty-six, which was for anti-aging and health benefits. How about you? Can you look deep within your soul at this time and think of any intentions you would like to create? My purpose for writing this chapter was to help you gain empowerment and identify your strengths and weaknesses. Remove your limited thinking. Too often we can't move in any direction because we don't have the money, the time, or the know-how. Maybe you have been a schoolteacher for 40 years, but as a teenager you desired to dance. It is never too late to do research on classes or other resources that may interest you.

When our local university jazz radio station was created, they were not playing any of the local jazz artists that lived in Nashville. I knew most of the local artists, so I called the station and asked them if they wanted me to introduce them to their music. The answer was yes. The artists have been thrilled with the newfound exposure and the station with the new inspiring music. Later I partnered up with a local DJ and we started to book bands at a local club. Next, I started writing for a local publication about the happenings and events in the jazz world, and I began to receive money from both the bookings and my writing. This was a burning desire to serve in love and passion. In return, everyone was blessed. The jazz community benefited from my new talent. One local gifted artist worked fulltime on another job and played music at night. He has created three jazz CDs and plays local clubs two or three nights a week. His music is born out of pure passion and a desire to play music. Change has now occurred on the Nashville jazz radio because of my desires. My confidence has grown because I gained insights to the music world and new skills. My soul's purpose was developed. Isn't that what life is all about? This was a skill I didn't realize I had until I applied my heart, spirit, and soul to it. Can you say yes? You never know what passion and soul's purpose will lead you into a real job with real money. Open your heart and walk the sacred path into a destiny. The intention of this chapter is to awaken your inner being and your soul's purpose. We all have many purposes. It's time to become empowered and proactive. Our talents, whatever they may be, are needed in our community.

There is a sweet spirited woman I know. She's faced cancer in her body for over twelve years in different areas of her body. Every day she reaches out and offers assistance to others with compassion in her heart. Many wonder where she gets her fortitude and positive attitude. She told me her passion and purpose is showing others the Christ within her. Even through her illness, she spreads light and love all around. Her motto is that you must laugh, laugh, and then laugh some more. She lost all her hair from the treatment of brain cancer and was told it may never grow back. She told the doctors, "I'd rather wear a wig the rest of my days than be lying in the ground." Her mission is to raise her son. She has been one of God's earth angels helping me with this book.

Our soul's purpose is to teach, share, and strengthen others who many need our assistance on their path. We need to live life to the fullest, making this earth our heaven. Have you seen something you can improve? List it here.

Are you going to sit back and do nothing?

Most people think that a preacher, nun, or someone who leads a church is the only one who can be called to serve. When my children were small in public schools, I worked with the PTA to provide leadership. Before I accepted the call as president of the PTA, I went to my church elders and they prayed for me.

Afterwards I knew that this was a calling from my sacred source. I had a blissful feeling of peace and clarity. You know when you are on purpose if you feel those things. What you are doing is right for you and all involved. I had a burning desire to use my gifts and talents a long time before this happened. I just answered the call to serve the community providing the leadership. The community at large was a better place. The missionaries at my church helped me with the work. There was daily joy in the service of the parents, children, and teachers. I pulled the parents together, even though they were from all walks of life. The task was so easy! When problems arose, we as a team always had a solution to combat it quickly, thanks to the Spirit's guidance and direction. I defined my mission.

You must know what is yours to do within your heart and soul. Then there will be no room for doubt and fear. Fears keep us from approaching and carrying out our intentions in our life. As a parents' group, what we set out to achieve as a team was accomplished within 4 months with God's help. There was never a day of service to that community or school that I did not give my all. Because I trusted in where my strength and my help come from and gave thanks, I was offered a job in the district. I worked as a parent consultant for 4 years. The school director let me develop my own concepts for parent involvement. The new school director was an open-minded leader who could see beyond labels and lack of education to people's talents. All the people who worked in administration had education degrees. So you can see that I was very blessed to create a parent involvement plan for the district.

I had creativity, purpose, intention, and know-how to answer the call to serve the community. Later an educational publisher called me and asked me to develop a parent involvement book for teachers based on my insights, my intentions, and my purpose. I published that book in 1996, *Parents Are Lifesavers*. While writing that book, I was awakened many times by a nudging to write. I could hear the script clearly. This was my destiny; my heart was open and full of a passion for what I was doing. I slept, ate, and breathed the work. Have you heard the call? Again I ask you, what have you been sensing? Have you felt a nudge, a pull toward particular things to develop or create? Often people who want to give or to serve think they can't do it in a church, school, community, or workplace. They think service can't be performed because no one gave them a personal phone call, letter, knock at their door, or brought them into an office to ask them.

If your spirit or soul is being drawn, directed, pulled, or nudged toward a particular effort, then it's calling your soul's destiny. In Chapter 4 we used a timely scripture for inspiration, Ecclesiastes 3:1, *"To everything there is a season, a time for every purpose under heaven."*

Don't wait for a call by someone to direct you. If I had waited for that person, I would have never used my gifts. I place true intention in my heart filled with love. Then I consult the
Universal God to see if this is where I may use my God given talents and abilities. Next,

I ask if it is the will of my sacred source, then I ask for direction. I seek knowledge, who, where, and how. Finally, I knock at God's door for the blessed opportunities to serve my fellow man on this earth."

Fear is one of the largest reasons for not achieving our purpose in life. How often when we want to approach or walk closer to our soul's destiny does the negative self talk or a voice from the past stir up in our soul? Fear is learned behavior that can be overcome by recognizing and developing courage to try something new, and by replacing fear with faith in God and in yourself. Transformation in your mind, heart, and soul is necessary for positive achievement. Your words within your head and in your speech will need to be renewed or changed to more positive affirmations such as: I can, I will, I do, and I must.

The inner work is just as important as the outside work on your body. Too often we allow the past of our soul's journey to stop us from continuing to improve our life's journey. The past is simply what it is – the past. Every morning when you awake it's all a new day and a fresh start. I have said this more than once; you owe it to your soul and to your creator to reinvent yourself and take steps for good on this earth. Many times I walked stepping stones to reinvent myself.

Every day the steps brought me to a higher path that slowly manifested itself. I kept my concepts of change in my head, a picture of how I wanted to look, where I wanted to go, and how I might get there. Each experience or newness brings you one step closer to bliss, assuredness, and clarity of your individual purpose and path. Stepping slowly on the stones of faith, belief, destiny, laughter, kindness, reliance, determination, and fortitude, your story will be revealed under the heavens as your true path.

You are free to use your will to serve your fellow man or to sit at home and do nothing. It's your choice. Passion is a choice. When I decided to get back into performing arts and opened my heart to the guidance of my sacred source, the windows and doors were opened up to me. Once I faced my inner demons and surrendered to the Universal God, my path became revealed. I know the best is yet to come. Don't compare yourself to others. Own what is yours to do with your life's destiny. Most of the time I am able to balance home, career, my social life, and children.

You may be able to do so too. My cousin has a big title job, but his and his wife's first priority is to put their children's needs first. They could have a big house and new cars, but they choose not to have those things. Their passion is their children's well-being. Their belief when they brought children into this world was that they owed them first priorities. He said once he is dead and gone, if his children just put on his tombstone "Good Loving Father," that's all that needs to be said. He could rest in peace.

Another friend of mine for many years put her family's needs before hers and taught her children a spiritual practice to use in their adult destiny. Her three children were gifted in dancing and performing arts. As they were growing up, she drove them to dance class every day. Looking on the outside, one would think that it all was a huge sacrifice, but it really was a big investment in the lives of her children, who are all grown now. One is an assistant professor of dance at a very prestigious college; another received a high school talent scholarship for dance at the age of 16. She now teaches dance at a dance company in a big city. The other daughter is living her destiny. She's a mother and homemaker. This love and passion is what she is called to at this time under the heavens. We all aren't put on earth to be in front of others, just like my friend. She was not to be on stage to be seen by an audience, but she was highly favored by her God, her family, and community. She's now a grandmother of two. Her and her husband's seeds have been planted and nurtured long before those grandbabies were born. The fruits of her time, means, and labor have paid off in her lifetime for her to witness. All that matters at the end of the day is that you live your life in love and with a full intent. When my children were growing up we kept them busy using their talents, skills, and abilities.

This was our plan.

Don't judge. Support and do for others who get lost on their path. Help them return. What's so important for all of us is that we return to ourselves and find our way again. This is only accomplished through our relationship with our sacred source and our willingness or desire. Destiny's calling all of us to serve at one time or another and opens our hearts to hear.

In the Stillness, Blessings Unfold

This, what I am writing to you, is the end of this book. I entered the national over-40 model search five months ago. Knowing that I would be doing this, I prepared myself daily for a year and a half with a spiritual practice, exercise, and healthy eating. In my kitchen, one wall is dedicated to my visions of performing and dreams of what I want in my life. I have cut pictures from magazines and elsewhere to remind me of the dream.

I didn't get a call on the deadline. Now what? For 18 months I formed a partnership with Spirit to make my dreams a reality. Do I give up to my emotions and never dream again? The week before the end of the contest, I felt my spirit and path were at a crossroad. God's promptings were preparing me for what I felt was my big letdown, as it appeared to me. I was feeling restless and anxious.

Here I was, a spiritual being having a big turbulent human experience like the winds and storms. One would say that life threw me a curve ball that hit me all over my body. At this point I could be driven into the dirt

and stay down. I thought I could try again
and try again to hit a home run
toward my destiny.

Have you ever wanted something so bad that
you would die for it? What was your feeling
when it didn't happen at the time you
thought appointed or like you thought it
should? While taking my grandbaby to see
her father in the Army in Georgia, I called
my friend to tell her that I didn't get the call.
It was now 5 p.m. in New York. Tears were
flowing down my face and I could barely
see to drive. She said, "Carol, your destiny
would not change if that's what you and
God wanted." She also said that maybe the
timing was off for me to compete in New
York at this time. My son said, "Mom, when
God allows one door to close, the Spirit then
opens up two or more other ones." He also
told me that there must be something greater
for me in the future; several well-wishers
told me that also. I just didn't want to hear
that thoughtful answer from them at that
time. Others told me that there were many
possibilities opened for me. When you are
facing a crossroad, it is easy to think that
you have no other options. You must
become

still and silent in order to gain an understanding of what is happening or where to go now.

Crossroads are simply just what they are: roads where decisions are made. You may go here or there, or over here and around those curves. Just cross one way or the other by making a conscious choice with your eyes wide open. There are many ways to achieve your goals. Asking for Spirit's divine help and guidance is where I started again. I just needed to be alone in the silence to make the right actions and hear the words of God. I just needed to open my heart, mind, and soul to go, move, or travel. At this time I needed to feel God's Spirit pulling me along because my own spirits were low. "Keep moving forward," Spirit said to me, minute by minute, day by day and so on.

I asked my dear friend to ponder my situation and I would call her in the morning. The reason I asked for help and inspiration is that I wasn't sure if I heard an answer from the Spirit because of my deep emotional pain of disappointment. In the silence again, I cried and prayed for an answer. While reading at 10:35 p.m., the Law of Attraction book, an answer of inspiration to me came: In order for me to be a lifestyle coach, I must understand and relay real experiences to help others in their understanding.

At that point I said to myself, I am not writing that down as an answer. I fell asleep crying. I didn't believe the answer could be so simple. Some of the things I can assist otherswith are recognizing their spiritual awareness within, their inner strengths, self-doubt, and fear of failures, their anxiety, and how to regroup when facing a crossroad in their own life. This book will help anyone on their journey of awakening their soul's purpose or destiny.

I woke up with a song on my mind that stayed with me all day long with tears streaming down my face. The song is still ringing throughout my spirit seven days later. We sing this song at the Unity Church. The song is called "Blessings," written by Dr. Judy Blackwelder. One line of the song says, "God's blessings are all around me; all is good if only I see. I have everything I need; God's blessings are around me. Thank you, God, for everything. Then a verse from the Bible was impressed upon my mind and heart, Philippians 4:13 *"I can do all things through Christ who strengthens me."* My strength comes from the Spirit that dwells within me, in order for me to achieve all I need and have done. I called my friend that morning. At 9:35 p.m. the night before, she got in her car from church with my question on her heart. She and I talked about the perceived curveball events from the game of life. My friend pointed out to me that I thought this was the only way to get to do what I wanted to do in my life; that's how I was let down. There I go again limiting my sacred source. I thought this was because of my age, 51.

This was a contest for my age group, and I didn't think there was another way to get noticed in New York or on a national level. Remember, this was my childhood dream from the time I was 12 years old. A thought came to her mind about me, that I called myself a lifestyle coach. I must have experience on the subject matter to coach others on their way in the game of life, trying to fulfill their life's purposes. It is all in God's timing that dreams and purposes will show up. We both received similar messages at the same time in different regions. The message was through the challenge, what appeared to be despair. I thought that in order to model in New York as a mature model, I must have experiences to share and teach others and be a model for them. The message wasn't a loud call from Spirit, but a whisper from God's spirit to ours. I saw myself working in New York and still do as of this day, walking down the streets of the Big Apple, on the runways of that fashion capital. I wanted the challenge and experience of this contest. It was my dream for 39 years. It was my goal and dream to share my artistic expressions with the world.

Thinking that this was my only way to achieve my dreams, I thought my fulfillment was lost. The next day I revisited my childhood in my mind. Carol, I said, what were your dreams? Right now I am my internal coach pushing myself along with help from my sacred source. Here's my list: mother lots of children; design clothing and jewelry; model and be in magazines; writing books; help, support, and listen to others; travel; and last of all, have a career. I sat and saw myself as an adult doing those things again in my mind, giving up the how it will happen and not controlling the desired outcome of the Law of Attraction. After three days of digesting and accepting my big letdown, I pondered my options of what do I do now, I didn't get the call?

They didn't call me from New York; what now? Someone told me that my disappointment was an opening for God's appointment. In the verse of "Blessings" it says again, "God's Blessings are all around me, if only I see." I thought about the word *see.* The dictionary's meaning is to perceive by the eye; to notice; to discover; to understand; to receive, to experience, to attend. To have the power of sight; to understand, to consider. In the old gospel song "Amazing Grace" a line goes, "Was blind, but now I see." Here is a list of my blessings as I examined my life now: I have a spiritual awareness; God's unlimited love for me; health and wellness; talents and abilities; my work as a massage therapist and the benefit of being self-employed that allows me my freedom; I teach and coach at a model/talent agency in Nashville; and a mother and friend to others. Trust and faith in the Holy Spirit's presence in my life and in the life of my love ones is what I witness daily. How often are we so blind that we just can't see the blessings from Spirit?

Today I take off my blinders and open my spiritual eyes. This is my new affirmation for me. I want the power of sight: to understand, to consider like the dictionary's meaning all that's only given if we are willing to allow Spirit to help us. My eyes are open to see the visions and dreams that God and I have co-designed for me even now. I know that God grants us the desires of our hearts in the right timing, no matter the age. God is unlimited and we share that unlimited power within. I thought about folding into life's curve ball; have you ever done that? I could look up, run home, stay there, and never come out to play ball again. U-turns are just that: turns that take you in another direction. I have not given up my childhood dreams of either being a model or working with people as a lifestyle coach on a national level. I will give up the how and when it's all supposed to happen for me. This is called surrendering and letting go. As I write this message to you I am open and creating other ways to achieve my destiny. What would you do if you were in my shoes and you felt close to your dreams and worked very hard to achieve them, but you aren't there yet on the level you desire? My new goals are to finish this book, teach/coach my students, be silent and still while I wait, and go to New York in a few months on my own and knock on doors. I am going to NYC! I will create my own experience. I want to still model and be in magazines. Regroup your mind and focus; rest your soul for a while in the silence. Use your spiritual practices that only you create and go into the silence, for your answers lay in the quite peace. Know and see your blessings in your life; list them. My goals that I started with in Chapters 1-2, I have strived for and attained my weight goal. I wear a size 4-6, not a 12. The goals and dreams in chapter 3, I have successfully achieved also. I have worked as a mature model in my hometown and teach performing arts. I had been in four music videos, three fashion shows, and a national commercial. I have a closet full of vintage and classic clothing. Chapter 4 talks about "In Due Season" and also about change and time. I trust God and have faith in the how and when in Spirit's timing. Everything in our lives changes and nothing stays the same, all in God's timing. We must wake up our minds because Destiny is calling our souls. Say yes. Blessings are around us if only we see.

While in the Silence one day, I asked my inner guidance, "How may I serve? Help me to see my way." I felt an inspiration to write an article about chapters 1 and 2 of this book. Telling my personal transformation, I sent the story off to five local publications. Within six hours, I had two respond that they wanted to share my story with their readers. They also requested before and after pictures for the viewers to see. The next day I pondered again, "How may I serve?" I went to the bookstore and bought five national magazines. After sending the story to them, within two hours a magazine publication in New York contacted me for permission to publish my story! They also requested pictures. Another local publication did the same. When I thought all was lost again, many doors were opened. I knew I wanted to be in a magazine and I am now, just in a different way. This is why you have to let go of how the way things turn out sometimes. My focus was on the over – 40 contest - thinking that this was the only way.

When one door is closed, many open up if you still hold on to the dream or vision. At the ending here, I am now being considered as a Lifestyle Model with a large agency. So,
dreams do come true after 39 years.
"Reason may fail you. If you are going to do anything in life, you sometimes have to move away from it, beyond all measurements. You must follow sometimes visions and dreams." Bede Jarrett, *The House of Gold*

About the Author:

Rev. Carol S. Batey, Ph.D. is the author of
Parents Are Lifesavers (Corwin Press,
1996), In Due Season: Destiny's Calling
Your Soul (Authorhouse, 2006), Poise for
the Runway of Your Life (Authorhouse,
2008), What's Cooking in Your Soul?
(Authorhouse, 2010) and Unlocking Your
Potential to Write Books (Available July
2011). She is committed to spreading
information about how one can improve and
renew the purpose of one's soul by
providing coaching workshops and speaking
at seminars for anyone who wants to step
into their destiny.

Carol has worked as a Parent Involvement
Consultant for the Metropolitan Nashville
(Tennessee) Public Schools and received
national recognition from educators for her
work on parent involvement. During the
1992 school year, she was nominated for the
J.C. Penny Golden Rule Award, an award is
given to individuals who have performed
outstanding service to the local community,
and the school won $1000.

Born and raised in Nashville, Tennessee,
Spiritual Lifestyle Coach is the mother of
six adult children, and the author of

numerous magazine and newspaper articles. Carol was educated in the Nashville Public schools system, and has obtained multiple Associate Degrees in business from various schools in Nashville and currently resides in Nashville, Tennessee.

Carol, at 53, is a Lifestyle Model for Elite Models in Atlanta and a talent of Sharon Smith Talent. She teaches and has worked in the performing arts on assignments. Her "Your Destiny Awaits You" workshops are very popular, and attendants leave with knowledge, motivation, and instruction and a sense of self-empowerment.

She welcomes your e-mails or personal calls, for speaking, coaching, retreats, or workshops for your organization or yourself. Contact Carol via carol37076@aol.com; (615)-485-4548; or her Web site: www.artlifestylecoach.com. Carol would like to know how this book impacts your life, world, and affairs.

If you are wanting a successful career in the performing arts, or simply a more successful life, Carol Batey is the spiritual life coach for you! Combining all the principles of *Intentional Creation* and *The Secret*, Carol's rich life experiences, thoughtfully and

clearly presented, are a living example of how to pursue a dream with amazing perseverance and clearly miraculous effort. She will take you through a body reformation, presentation, resolution of family dilemmas, and life review to find and succeed at your special destiny. Her beauty at age 50 is matched only by the beauty of her mind and soul in pursuing her dreams and making them a reality. Enjoy the rich inspiration that she offers and apply everything she says for a total makeover in creating your next reality! Dr. Louise Mallory-Elliott, Spiritual Mentor, Teacher, and Healer Carol Batey speaks to the trinity within all of us. Her words offer healing for body, mind and spirit. She not only shares her personal story, but also gives her readers clear and effective steps to awaken their own soul's purpose, reminding them that it will unfold in due season.
-- Rev. Denise Yeargin, Unity Church for Positive Living, Old Hickory, Tennessee

In Due Season is a unique autobiographical account echoing the simple-to-hear yet difficult-to-act-upon message that we all have special gifts, and we were put here on this earth to share those gifts to help our friends, our loved ones, our communities, and most of all, ourselves, by finding and

following our passion in life. Carol shares her intimate journey throughout her life: how she traded fear for passion and drove her passion with faith. It is a refreshing text, which reminds us all that true happiness does not come from external material things, but rather, from within—by discovering one's purpose and steadfastly pursuing it.
—Michael Fair, Nashville Smooth Jazz Recording Artist

In Due Season is a fascinating read – an intimate tale of one woman's personal journey to self-expression, with God's Spirit as her ever-present guide. In the face of challenge after challenge, Carol Batey bounces back with grit and determination, never losing sight of her purpose in life. In truth, she serves a larger purpose than she may realize in sharing her joys and sorrows, her secrets about listening to and learning from her own inner guidance. I highly recommend the book to those eager to learn how to find and express their purpose in life, as they awaken to the Guide within.
– Bea Leff, Unity Ministerial Student

WOW! AWESOME! MOVING! THOUGHT PROVOKING! SPIRITUAL! REFRESHING!

Carol Batey has hit all the points in her compelling, open discussion about how we can move into our destiny. She has illustrated both the physical and the mental recipe for a life of peace and joy by living in faith, through the "Word of God." She has shared her own personal experiences to vividly bring to life her message to the readers. This is a book not just for those in the field of Performance Arts, but for everyone, for life is a real live performance with many Acts, and God is watching us all.

-- Sherrell F. Batey, Teacher, Inspirational Speaker, Theology Student

I have known Carol Batey as a massage therapist for several years and have witnessed the amazing change in her. Batey's book tells her story much as she told portions of it to me during our sessions. If I had to choose just one line from her book for inspiration, it would be, *I am my best supporter!* That affirmation hit me in the face. Too often I have crippled myself waiting for approval from others. Carol is living proof that the plan in the book works. Hers are tough footprints to follow—but look where she is today!

-- Jeannie Seely, Grand Ole Opry Entertainer

Proof

Made in the USA
Charleston, SC
09 April 2011